SUPERNATURAL

Living In The Power Of The Holy Spirit.

Paul E Chapman

SUPERNATURAL

Living In The Power Of The Holy Spirit.

By Paul E Chapman

All Scriptures are from the King James Version.

Published by:
Add To Your Faith Publications
P.O. Box 5369
S. Kingstown, RI, USA

Copies Available At AddToYourFaith.com.

Printed in USA

Let's Connect...

You can connect with me by subscribing to updates at **PaulEChapman.com** and following me on social media platforms by searching the handle **@thepaulechapman**.

I look forward to getting to know you!

1

We Are Supernatural

Supernatural. What an exciting word!

It is commonly used in American culture today. Some people use it to describe fictional heroes promoted by Marvel or DC Comics that have been featured in books and movies. Other folks use it (especially around Halloween) to describe spirits, ghouls, and goblins. Yet, the word supernatural means so much more!

Did you know that you are supernatural? It's true!

God created you as a supernatural being. More importantly, through the Holy Spirit, our Saviour grants us access to live in an increasingly supernatural way as we surrender to Him.

I pray that through this book you will learn the depth of the supernatural gifts you have been given and the heights of the supernatural life that you can attain.

What does the word supernatural mean?

The adjective super is from the Latin "super" meaning "above," "over," or "beyond."

Merriam-Webster Dictionary defines the adjective form of super as *"1. of high grade or quality. 2. very large or powerful. 3. exhibiting the characteristics of its top to an extreme or excessive degree."* These definitions are self-evident in words such as superintendent, supercar, superheat, superhighway, etc.

When you add the prefix "super-" to the word "natural," you enter the realm of the spiritual.

Consider *Merriam-Webster's* definition of the word supernatural.

> *1: of or relating to an order of existence beyond the visible observable universe*
>
> *especially : of or relating to God or a god, demigod, spirit, or devil.*
>
> *2a: departing from what is usual or normal especially so as to appear to transcend the laws of nature.*
>
> *b: attributed to an invisible agent (such as a ghost or spirit).*

Synonyms of "supernatural" include metaphysical, otherworldly, paranormal, preternatural, transcendent, transcendental, and unearthly.

The word supernatural refers to something beyond the natural – things which natural laws cannot explain. It refers to something "more" than natural.

Take a moment to look around you now. What do you see? All of it is natural. The natural world can be seen, touched, tasted, heard, or smelled. It can be easily understood. But what lies beyond what you can see? There is an unseen spiritual world at work all around us all the time. It is invisible. It is eternal.

It is supernatural.

Look at your hands. Your body exists in the natural world. Yet, God created you in His image as a triune being. You have a body, a soul, and a spirit.

> *1 Thessalonians 5:23*
>
> *"And the very God of peace sanctify you wholly; and I pray God your whole spirit and soul and body be preserved blameless unto the coming of our Lord Jesus Christ."*

The body exists in the natural world, but your soul and spirit are spiritual.

They are supernatural.

As a human, you exist in both worlds. You have a natural body and a supernatural soul. You are able to experience the natural world and the supernatural world simultaneously. What a gift!

Sadly, most people only focus on the natural world. Our culture is becoming increasingly naturalistic, focusing only on what they can observe and explain.

Here is a big reason why.

Science began as an exploration into our natural world to explain the supernatural. Robert Boyle (1627-1691) was a prominent scientist who argued that the study of science could improve the glory of God. Justus von Liebig (1803-1873) was a celebrated chemist who said, *"The greatness and infinite wisdom of the Creator will be recognized only by those who really endeavor to draw their ideas from the great book we call nature."*

Isaac Newton was a noted English scientist and innovator in the fields of mathematics, optics, and mechanics.

He considered numbers as the path to understanding God's designs. Galileo looked to the stars to learn about the Creator. He said, *"Mathematics is the language with which God has written the universe."* People studied what they could see to learn about our Maker and how He created the universe.

Over time, men of science became full of themselves. They were so impressed with their own intellect and accomplishments that they began to worship themselves rather than the Creator.

Impious people looked for a way to detach humanity from their Maker. They conjectured that if there was no Creator, then there was no accountability or standard of morality. In the absence of God, mankind could be a god.

The theory of evolution finally gave people a way to explain away faith.

Although Darwin himself still believed in God, his theory led others to believe that the universe could be created without God. Even though the theory of evolution has many variations and is always evolving itself, it is usually presented as a fact.

Since the Scopes trial of 1925, evolution has been taught almost exclusively in America's educational system. This focus on naturalism has taken hold in the culture. Some scientists today go so far as to doubt the existence of anything supernatural.

They reason (falsely) that if they can't see it or understand something, then it must not exist. Imagine the pride required to believe that!

The result of this separation of mankind from his supernatural roots has been catastrophic. Billions of sinners flounder in mediocrity and malaise with no hope, peace, or joy.

Unbelievers look to natural elements such as amusement,

accomplishment, and addiction to fill the void.

Multitudes flounder in godless lives stumbling about in spiritual darkness.

Natural medications are prescribed for spiritual problems in a futile attempt to fix them. Depression, anger, immorality, and suicide are all on the rise in a world with no knowledge of a Saviour to defeat them. Worst of all, the broad way leading to eternal destruction is crowded with lost souls stumbling into a supernatural Hell they don't even know exists.

We must return to our supernatural roots. Christians must understand their place in the supernatural, reminding the world of its existence and consequence.

Let's consider three reasons why the supernatural is important in your life and how embracing it will make your life infinitely better.

1. God is supernatural .

John 4:21–24

"Jesus saith unto her, Woman, believe me, the hour cometh, when ye shall neither in this mountain, nor yet at Jerusalem, worship the Father. Ye worship ye know not what: we know what we worship: for salvation is of the Jews. But the hour cometh, and now is, when the true worshippers shall worship the Father in spirit and in truth: for the Father seeketh such to worship him. God is a Spirit: and they that worship him must worship him in spirit and in truth."

The Bible is clear that God exists as a Trinity. God is One Being Who exists in three co-equal persons. God the Father, God the Son, and God the Holy Spirit exist together in perfect all-powerful harmony.

God the Father is a Spirit. God the Holy Spirit is (obviously) a Spirit. Jesus Christ is the part of the Trinity that has a body. He was clothed in flesh and become a perfect man to live as man and die for men. Here's what the Bible says.

Colossians 2:8–10

"Beware lest any man spoil you through philosophy and vain deceit, after the tradition of men, after the rudiments of the world, and not after Christ. For in him dwelleth all the fulness of the Godhead bodily. And ye are complete in him, which is the head of all principality and power:"

Jesus Christ is the member of the Godhead Who is mentioned to have form.

The Old Testament appearances of God are called Christophanies. They were Christ appearing as God.

God the Father is seen in the Old Testament as the fire and noise on Mt. Sinai.

God the Holy Spirit is seen in the New Testament in the form of a dove at the baptism of Christ and the flaming tongues of fire at Pentecost.

Usually, when you "see" God take form in Scripture it is in the person of Jesus Christ.

God is supernatural. He exists above and beyond the natural laws of our world. He is eternal, existing outside of time. He is all-powerful, operating without confinement to men and nature. He is omniscient, knowing all there is to know.

He is the Creator of everything. He is the Judge of everyone. He is the Beginning and the End. He is supernatural!

2. Man is supernatural.

God created us in His image as triune beings. We have a body, soul, and spirit.

We have uniquely spiritual nature that makes us special among God's creation. Animals don't have a soul or a spirit. God's spirit communicates with man's spirit.

1 Corinthians 2:10–12

"But God hath revealed them unto us by his Spirit: for the Spirit searcheth all things, yea, the deep things of God. For what man knoweth the things of a man, save the spirit of man which is in him? even so the things of God knoweth no man, but the Spirit of God. Now we have received, not the spirit of the world, but the spirit which is of God; that we might know the things that are freely given to us of God."

Mankind has a unique place in Creation. We have a natural body and a supernatural soul.

The Biblical account of man's creation in Genesis chapter 2 explains this division.

Genesis 2:7

"And the LORD God formed man of the dust of the ground, and breathed into his nostrils the breath of life; and man became a living soul."

The Creator formed man's body out of the dust of the ground. This is the natural body. It is made of nature and is bound to this world. However, this body was a dead husk. What God did next was supernatural. He breathed His holy breath into the empty shell, and the dead body became a living soul!

Now the human body has a soul and spirit.

While our bodies are anchored to this world, our souls transcend it. Our souls are eternal.

Our soul can be saved and go to Heaven, but our bodies cannot go to Heaven.

7

That's why death is the doorway to Heaven. Physical death is simply the separation of the earthly bodies from our eternal souls.

Our natural bodies must die to release our supernatural souls.

Once our souls get to Heaven, we receive a celestial body that is not anchored to this world. It will be a supernatural body capable of eternal life and not bound to the natural laws of this world.

> *1 Corinthians 15:44*
>
> *"It is sown a natural body; it is raised a spiritual body. There is a natural body, and there is a spiritual body."*

There will be one generation who goes to Heaven without dying. Those who are alive during the Rapture will have their bodies supernaturally transformed into a heavenly body in the twinkling of an eye.

> *1 Corinthians 15:50–52*
>
> *"Now this I say, brethren, that flesh and blood cannot inherit the kingdom of God; neither doth corruption inherit incorruption. Behold, I shew you a mystery; We shall not all sleep, but we shall all be changed, In a moment, in the twinkling of an eye, at the last trump: for the trumpet shall sound, and the dead shall be raised incorruptible, and we shall be changed."*

My friend, you are supernatural!

3. God calls us to a supernatural life.

We are eternal beings existing in natural bodies. We are currently restrained to the laws of the universe and the predisposition of our DNA. However, we are not bound by them completely. Through the Holy Spirit, we can rise above our fleshly instincts. God can empower us to live beyond normal human abilities.

We are commanded to be filled with the Spirit.

Ephesians 5:18

"And be not drunk with wine, wherein is excess; but be filled with the Spirit;"

Alcohol in wine changes the personality and character of its abuser. In a similar manner, the Holy Spirit energizes the person He fills to engage the mind and character of Christ.

The fullness of the Holy Spirit makes us better in every way possible.

Also, we are commanded to walk in the Spirit and display His fruit. We will learn how to be filled with the Spirit and to walk in Him in the following chapters of this book.

Galatians 5:16–18

"This I say then, Walk in the Spirit, and ye shall not fulfil the lust of the flesh. For the flesh lusteth against the Spirit, and the Spirit against the flesh: and these are contrary the one to the other: so that ye cannot do the things that ye would. But if ye be led of the Spirit, ye are not under the law."

We can be like Jesus. We can have His mind to think as He thinks. We can have His heart to feel as He fills. We can have His power to rise above the craziness of this world. We can have His strength to transform lives.

God is supernatural. We are supernatural. It's time to start living like it.

This book will show us how to step into our supernatural potential and become more than we ever dreamed possible.

Are you ready? Let's begin.

2

Introduction To The Holy Spirit

The Holy Spirit is at work in your life every day. Let's take a few minutes to learn Who He is and what He does.

What is the Holy Spirit?

Who is the Holy Spirit?

What does He do?

Have you ever asked these questions?

You need to know the Holy Spirit. He is at work in your life today, seeking to empower you to greatness. You can surrender to His ministry, doing more than you ever dreamed, or you can resist His work, staying chained to mediocrity.

The Holy Spirit is given 15 different titles in the Bible. The most common are Holy Spirit, Spirit, and Holy Ghost. The Holy Spirit is mentioned in the New Testament in 261 verses. God intends for the Holy Spirit to be a large part of your life, empowering you to live supernaturally every day.

There is some confusion in Christian circles regarding the Holy Spirit. I believe there are three prominent reasons for this confusion.

1. Some churches don't teach the doctrine of the Holy Spirit.

A lack of emphasis and explanation of this vital doctrine leaves an alarming number of professing believers with very little knowledge of our Comforter. In Acts 19:2, the Apostle Paul ran into people that had been baptized by John the Baptist but had never even heard of the Holy Ghost.

> *Acts 19:2*
>
> *"He said unto them, Have ye received the Holy Ghost since ye believed? And they said unto him, We have not so much as heard whether there be any Holy Ghost."*

I have met Christians today who know little to nothing about the Holy Spirit Who dwells within them. How sad!

2. Some denominations teach false doctrines regarding the Holy Spirit.

These false teachers misinterpret the Scriptures to make the Spirit into something He is not. We will cover some of these false doctrines in later chapters.

Don't miss this important truth. The Holy Spirit does not bring attention to Himself. Even though the Bible has a tremendous amount of information about Him, the Spirit usually works in the background, veiling Himself behind Christ.

The Holy Spirit promotes Christ rather than speak of Himself. This fact doesn't make the Holy Spirit less important, but it can cause confusion if you don't rightly divide the Word of Truth.

12

John 16:13

"Howbeit when he, the Spirit of truth, is come, he will guide you into all truth: for he shall not speak of himself; but whatsoever he shall hear, that shall he speak: and he will shew you things to come."

Jesus Christ taught His disciples the importance of the Holy Spirit's ministry in John chapters fourteen through sixteen.

John 15:26

"But when the Comforter is come, whom I will send unto you from the Father, even the Spirit of truth, which proceedeth from the Father, he shall testify of me: "

The significance of the ministry of the Spirit cannot be overstated. Nevertheless, if any Christian or group emphasizes the Holy Ghost more than Christ, they are in the weeds of false doctrine.

3. Some preachers avoid the subject of the Holy Spirit.

In an unfortunate, knee-jerk reaction to Christian groups who misuse the doctrine of the Spirit, some preachers ignore Him in their teaching ministry. These ministers rarely talk about the Spirit unless it is to refute the false doctrines of other groups. The average Christian in his church knows very little about the sweet Holy Ghost.

As a result, the Christian life becomes a hard slog attempted in the power of the flesh by believers who never experience sweet fellowship with the Spirit.

All three circumstances mentioned here are tragic. Christians must learn the beautiful truths in God's Word about the Holy Spirit! If the Devil separates God's people from the power of the Holy Spirit, he essentially neutralizes our effectiveness for Christ in this world.

My Introduction To The Holy Spirit.

I was blessed to be saved in a healthy church that thoroughly taught all that the Bible had to say about the Holy Spirit. Certainly, Pastor Ross refuted the false doctrines of the various sects regarding the Holy Spirit. However, he also taught us the futility of trying to live the Christian life in the power of the flesh. He taught us to be filled with the Spirit and to walk in Him daily.

I will be forever grateful for the sound doctrine I was taught through the Blessed Hope Baptist Church of Jasonville, Indiana.

Furthermore, I was introduced to great preachers and evangelists of the past who displayed the power of the Holy Ghost through earthshaking ministries. They shook nations, impacted popular culture, and changed the course of history as they were filled with the Holy Spirit. Men from all walks of life and various abilities ministered in the mighty power of God.

As a young man I began to thirst for the Spirit-filled life. I have spent 30 years on a journey with the sweet Holy Ghost as my constant Companion and Friend. I have much to learn of Him still.

I pray that this book will be used by the Lord to help you to know the Holy Ghost better and bring Christ much glory as the Spirit fills you to new levels of power in service.

As we are introduced to the the Holy Spirit, let's consider six important facts.

1. The Holy Spirit Is A Person.

Ephesians 4:30

"And grieve not the holy Spirit of God, whereby ye are sealed unto the day of redemption."

Some people believe wrongly that the Holy Spirit is an impersonal force. They teach that He is not a person, but an unthinking energy.

Nothing could be further from the truth! The Bible is clear that the Holy Spirit is a person. He thinks. He feels. He loves. He grieves. He speaks. He moves.

God, the Holy Spirit, is a member of the Godhead with thoughts, will, and emotion like God the Father and God the Son.

2. The Holy Spirit Is Omnipotent.

Genesis 1:2

"And the earth was without form, and void; and darkness was upon the face of the deep. And the Spirit of God moved upon the face of the waters."

The Holy Spirit is all-powerful. The Word of God introduces the Spirit in the second verse of Scripture. We see Him immediately using His awesome power in the creation of the world. His omnipotence is declared repeatedly in Scripture as He accomplishes miracles.

3. The Holy Spirit Is Omnipresent.

Psalm 139:7

"Whither shall I go from thy spirit? Or whither shall I flee from thy presence? "

The Holy Spirit is not bound by time or space. His power is not limited by distance. He is everywhere at the same time.

4. The Holy Spirit Is Omniscient.

1 Corinthians 2:10–11

"But God hath revealed them unto us by his Spirit: for the Spirit searcheth all things, yea, the deep things of God. For what man knoweth the things of a man, save the spirit of man which is in him? even so the things of God knoweth no man, but the Spirit of God."

The Holy Spirit is all-knowing. He has all knowledge. Nothing is hidden from Him. He knows all there is to know about us. As God, He knows everything that God knows. He reveals the unsearchable riches of Scripture to the children of God.

5. The Holy Spirit Is God.

Acts 5:3–4

"But Peter said, Ananias, why hath Satan filled thine heart to lie to the Holy Ghost, and to keep back part of the price of the land?

Whiles it remained, was it not thine own? and after it was sold, was it not in thine own power? why hast thou conceived this thing in thine heart? thou hast not lied unto men, but unto God."

The Holy Spirit is God. He is an inseparable member of the eternal Godhead. He is equal with the Father and Son.

Consider this verse.

Matthew 28:19-20

"Go ye therefore, and teach all nations, baptizing them in the name of the Father, and of the Son, and of the Holy Ghost: Teaching them to observe all things whatsoever I have commanded you: and, lo, I am with you alway, even unto the end of the world. Amen."

The Holy Bible speaks of the Holy Ghost as equal with the Father and the Son. He is God.

6. The Holy Spirit Is Busy.

Romans 15:19

"Through mighty signs and wonders, by the power of the Spirit of God; so that from Jerusalem, and round about unto Illyricum, I have fully preached the gospel of Christ."

The Holy Spirit empowered Paul to do the work of God. The Spirit is always seen in Scripture as working and moving. He is the engine of all spiritual activity in us.

We have identified 34 activities of the Holy Ghost in the life of the believer. This doesn't include his ministries in other areas.

Yes, the Holy Spirit is busy. In fact, He is working on you right now. He is teaching you the eternal truth of God through the Scripture in this book and revealing Himself to you in a new and exciting way.

Whether you realize it or not, the Holy Spirit is constantly working in your life in supernatural ways.

As you learn more about Him and His ability to empower you, you will become more like Christ and more effective in the Kingdom of God.

We will build upon this short introduction to the Holy Ghost throughout this book. Soon, you will be convinced that the sweet Holy Spirit is one of the greatest gifts God has bestowed upon His children.

3

Our Relationship With The Holy Spirit

What is your relationship with the Holy Spirit? How would you describe it? Or do you even have one?

Some professed believers are not even aware of the Holy Spirit! Acts chapter 19 conveys a story in which the Apostle Paul found disciples that had never heard of the Holy Ghost.

Acts 19:1–2

"And it came to pass, that, while Apollos was at Corinth, Paul having passed through the upper coasts came to Ephesus: and finding certain disciples,

He said unto them, Have ye received the Holy Ghost since ye believed? And they said unto him, We have not so much as heard whether there be any Holy Ghost."

Sadly, some Christian denominations have misinterpreted and abused the doctrine of the Holy Spirit. We can't allow the fear of false doctrine to ruin our biblical understanding of the Holy Ghost. Additionally, some pastors seem to ignore the Person and work of the Spirit altogether. If the pastors and churches are not teaching the Bible doctrine of the Holy Spirit, most of their churchgoers will not experience the blessing and power that God has designed for them.

The Holy Spirit indwells believers at the moment of salvation. He is Christ in us, the Hope of Glory. He is our source of spiritual strength. We cannot overstate His importance in our lives.

The Holy Spirit is the source of our power from God. The Holy Spirit accomplishes everything God is doing in you and through you.

The Holy Spirit is the source of our connection with God. He is God with us. He connects us to the Almighty through our spirits.

Sadly, most Christians feel more connected to their pets than to the blessed Holy Spirit.

This trend must change immediately!

God wants us to have a meaningful relationship with the Holy Spirit. He is a Person with thoughts, feelings, and intentions Who never leaves you.

He is meant to be our Comforter and Guide. Stop ignoring Him!

I'm grateful that I had pastors who taught me what the Bible says about the Holy Spirit. They encouraged me to get to know Him, seeking His fullness and power.

I do not claim to know all there is about the Holy Spirit. I do not share these truths with you as the ultimate practitioner of this incredible doctrine. I have not arrived, but I do seek after a meaningful relationship with the Holy Spirit. I am not a guru or master, but I do know what it's like to hear His still small voice. I have experienced His astounding power.

I know what it's like to:

- sense His presence.
- be comforted by His love.
- be strengthened by His grace.
- listen to His instruction.
- follow His leading.
- be filled with His power.

Unfortunately, I also know what it is like to be spiritually empty, filled with self and pride. Sadly, I have quenched His power and grieved His holy heart. I have ignored His promptings and resisted His guidance.

Forgive me, Lord.

There is no failure so complete as a believer trying to live like Christ in the power of the flesh. There is nothing more sad than a Christian trying to do the supernatural work of God in His own power.

I have not arrived, but I am on a lifelong journey to know what is means to be filled with the Spirit and exhibit His power. For over thirty years, I have traveled the road of life with my blessed Companion.

I want you to get to know Him personally.

Allow me to share with you some things I've learned along the way and how you can cultivate a personal, powerful relationship with the Holy Spirit.

Jesus Christ promised to leave us a Comforter.

Christ was preparing the disciples for His upcoming return to Heaven. Our Lord introduces the Holy Spirit as the Person of the Godhead Who would remain with them in His absence. He would be their Comforter, or Divine Helper, as they continued the holy mission to spread the Word and win souls.

John 14:16–18

"And I will pray the Father, and he shall give you another Comforter, that he may abide with you for ever; Even the Spirit of truth; whom the world cannot receive, because it seeth him not, neither knoweth him: but ye know him; for he dwelleth with you, and shall be in you. I will not leave you comfortless: I will come to you."

Christ dwells in us through the Person of the Holy Ghost.

Notice that Christ said in John 3:18, "I will come to you." Christ would come to the disciples in the Person of the Holy Spirit. The Holy Spirit is a co-equal, co-existent member of the Godhead. Since the Father, Son, and Holy Ghost are coequal, to have one is to have all the others. The Holy Spirit is "Christ in us."

Colossians 1:27

"To whom God would make known what is the riches of the glory of this mystery among the Gentiles; which is Christ in you, the hope of glory:"

Christ explained that it was better for us right now that He go back to Heaven and leave us the Holy Spirit.

John 16:7

"Nevertheless I tell you the truth; It is expedient for you that I go away: for if I go not away, the Comforter will not come unto you; but if I depart, I will send him unto you."

22

What an incredible statement! As the perfect man, Christ was limited to a place and time. Our Lord knew that when He ascended back into Heaven, the Holy Spirit would be with all believers at the same time. Christ could teach those who are present physically, but the Holy Spirit could teach anyone who would open their hearts. Our Saviour could only comfort those within His reach, but the Holy Ghost would comfort all believers.

Like many believers, I have often wished that Christ was here with me, that I could see His face and hear His voice. In God's perfect plan, however, we learn that the Holy Spirit is a greater gift than if we had our Lord here with us physically. That fact is hard to wrap our minds around.

Jesus declared that it was better for all of us that He go to Heaven and the Holy Spirit come.

Wow! We cannot overstate the importance of the Holy Spirit in our lives.

Our Lord explained that ministry efforts would be in vain unless the Holy Spirit worked through us.

Luke 24:46–49

"And said unto them, Thus it is written, and thus it behoved Christ to suffer, and to rise from the dead the third day: And that repentance and remission of sins should be preached in his name among all nations, beginning at Jerusalem. And ye are witnesses of these things. And, behold, I send the promise of my Father upon you: but tarry ye in the city of Jerusalem, until ye be endued with power from on high."

We are called to supernatural work. God's work deals with souls and spirits. Fleshly efforts and flowery language cannot change the heart or save a soul.

Spiritual work can only be accomplished through the power of the Holy Spirit.

The power of the Holy Spirit changes us. It bestows boldness, wisdom, and power needed to become powerful servants of God.

Acts 1:8

"But ye shall receive power, after that the Holy Ghost is come upon you: and ye shall be witnesses unto me both in Jerusalem, and in all Judaea, and in Samaria, and unto the uttermost part of the earth."

We need the Spirit's power to enable us to perform God's work. We are not equipped for spiritual battle until we are endued with power from on High.

Luke 24:49

"And, behold, I send the promise of my Father upon you: but tarry ye in the city of Jerusalem, until ye be endued with power from on high."

The Holy Spirit indwells the believer at the moment of salvation.

John 14:17

"Even the Spirit of truth; whom the world cannot receive, because it seeth him not, neither knoweth him: but ye know him; for he dwelleth with you, and shall be in you."

The Holy Spirit in us is our unbreakable connection to God and the source of His supernatural work in us and through us.

Ephesians 1:13–14

"In whom ye also trusted, after that ye heard the word

of truth, the gospel of your salvation: in whom also after that ye believed, ye were sealed with that holy Spirit of promise, Which is the earnest of our inheritance until the redemption of the purchased possession, unto the praise of his glory."

When the Spirit moved in, we became the temple of God! God dwells within us!

1 Corinthians 6:19–20

"What? know ye not that your body is the temple of the Holy Ghost which is in you, which ye have of God, and ye are not your own? For ye are bought with a price: therefore glorify God in your body, and in your spirit, which are God's".

There are two states of the Holy Ghost in the life of a believer mentioned in Scripture.

1. We Can Be FILLED With The Spirit.

Ephesians 5:18

"And be not drunk with wine, wherein is excess; but be filled with the Spirit;"

We are commanded to be filled with the Spirit. We can know we are filled with the Spirit.

A young man once asked an older preacher, "How can I know if I am filled with the Spirit?" Leaning in uncomfortably close and looking deep into the man's eyes, the aged preacher said, "You look about a quart low."

Our words, actions, and spiritual accomplishments are the proof of the Spirit's fullness. Consider the following by-products of being filled with the Holy Spirit.

- the Holy Spirit bears witness with our Spirit.

25

- transformation into another man.
- boldness for soul winning.
- power in ministry.
- fruit of the Spirit.
- lives characterized by Ephesians chapter five and six.

You will learn more about being filled with the Spirit in an upcoming chapter.

2. We Can Be NOT FILLED with the Spirit.

Either we are filled with the Holy Spirit, or we are not.

If we are not filled with the Holy Spirit, it is because we have committed one of the seven sins against him.

You will learn more about the seven sins against the Holy Spirit in an upcoming chapter.

When we reject the Spirit's work in our lives, we lose all the benefits of His activity. We have identified 34 activities of the Holy Ghost in the life of a believer. Some of these activities happened before salvation and helped bring us to Christ. Some of these activities happened at salvation when we were born again. Most of these activities are taking place now after our salvation as we live the Christian life.

There is a chapter on each of these three categories of the Spirit's work in our lives. For now, it is important to know that we lose the benefits of the Spirit's activities when we are not filled with Him.

A strong relationship with the Holy Spirit equals a better life and more productive ministry.

Galatians 5:16

"This I say then, Walk in the Spirit, and ye shall not fulfil the lust of the flesh."

Walking in the Spirit provides supernatural power to overcome the lusts of the flesh and display the fruit of the Spirit. It enables supernatural power for spiritual service. It imparts the character of Christ. It confers divine ability to live like the Master and make an eternal difference.

Spirit-fullness improves every area of our lives. It makes us better in every way. It enhances every relationship. Fullness of the Holy Spirit makes our lives better.

Why would we want to live without it?

Only through the fullness of the Holy Ghost can we hope to fulfill God's purpose for our lives. Are you filled with the Holy Spirit? How would you describe your relationship with the Holy Spirit right now?

Practice these simple habits to have a better relationship with the Holy Spirit.

- Be aware of His indwelling.
- Sense His presence.
- Listen for His still small voice.
- Yield to him often.
- Submit to His correction.
- Pray for His filling.

Take every opportunity to serve the Lord, trusting the Holy Spirit to empower you.

How would you describe your relationship with the Holy Spirit? Surely, there is room for improvement.

Begin your journey to a closer relationship with Him today.

4

The Baptism Of The Holy Ghost

Matthew 3:11

"I indeed baptize you with water unto repentance: but he that cometh after me is mightier than I, whose shoes I am not worthy to bear: he shall baptize you with the Holy Ghost, and with fire:"

Some use the terms anointing, baptism, and filling interchangeably when discussing the Holy Spirit. Actually, the Bible teaches that they are three different doctrines.

In this chapter, we will explore what the Bible says about the Baptism Of The Holy Ghost.

<u>THERE ARE 4 TYPES OF BAPTISM IN THE BIBLE:</u>

1. BAPTISM OF SURRENDER

This was the baptism of repentance performed by John the Baptist.

Acts 19:4

"Then said Paul, John verily baptized with the baptism of repentance, saying unto the people, that they should believe on him which should come after him, that is, on Christ Jesus."

2. BAPTISM OF THE SPIRIT

This baptism the subject of the chapter.

Matthew 3:11

"I indeed baptize you with water unto repentance: but he that cometh after me is mightier than I, whose shoes I am not worthy to bear: he shall baptize you with the Holy Ghost, and with fire:"

3. BAPTISM OF THE SAINTS

This is the baptism of believers after salvation.

Acts 8:36–37

"And as they went on their way, they came unto a certain water: and the eunuch said, See, here is water; what doth hinder me to be baptized? And Philip said, If thou believest with all thine heart, thou mayest. And he answered and said, I believe that Jesus Christ is the Son of God."

4. BAPTISM OF SUFFERING

Christ taught that all believers would suffer.

Matthew 20:22–23

"But Jesus answered and said, Ye know not what ye ask. Are ye able to drink of the cup that I shall drink of, and to be baptized with the baptism that I am baptized with? They say unto him, We are able. And he saith unto them,

Ye shall drink indeed of my cup, and be baptized with the baptism that I am baptized with: but to sit on my right hand, and on my left, is not mine to give, but it shall be given to them for whom it is prepared of my Father. "

What about the verse in the Bible that says there is one baptism? Does it disprove the idea of multiple types of baptism in the Bible? Not at all.

The "one baptism" in this verse speaks of believer's baptism.

Ephesians 4:4–6

"There is one body, and one Spirit, even as ye are called in one hope of your calling; One Lord, one faith, one baptism, One God and Father of all, who is above all, and through all, and in you all."

Although we are focusing on the baptisms mentioned in the New Testament, there were many baptisms under the Old Testament law, also. Clearly, there are multiple types of baptisms in the Bible.

Ephesians 4:4-6 urges Christian unity because we have these things listed in common.

Every committed believer has been baptized the same way - immersed in water in the name of the Father, Son, and Holy Ghost. This acts out our faith in Christ.

By this single act, Christians demonstrate their spiritual unity.

Now, let's focus on the baptism of the Holy Ghost.

The baptism of the Holy Ghost is a gift to New Testament Christians. It is a privilege because of Christ's finished payment for our sin.

What is the Baptism of the Holy Ghost?

Consider two important elements of this spiritual baptism:

A. We are baptized by the Spirit into Christ's death & resurrection.

Romans 6:3–4

"Know ye not, that so many of us as were baptized into Jesus Christ were baptized into his death? Therefore we are buried with him by baptism into death: that like as Christ was raised up from the dead by the glory of the Father, even so we also should walk in newness of life. "

Colossians 2:12

"Buried with him in baptism, wherein also ye are risen with him through the faith of the operation of God, who hath raised him from the dead."

Since we died with Christ, we are risen from the dead with Him!

B. We Are Baptized into Christ's Body at salvation.

1 Corinthians 12:13

"For by one Spirit are we all baptized into one body, whether we be Jews or Gentiles, whether we be bond or free; and have been all made to drink into one Spirit."

What is the body of Christ? We are - the Church!

1 Corinthians 12:27

"Now ye are the body of Christ, and members in particular."

Colossians 1:18

"And he is the head of the body, the church: who is the beginning, the firstborn from the dead; that in all things he might have the preeminence."

Is this baptism into the body of Christ referring to the universal, invisible church or the local, visible church?

Universal Church vs. Local Church

The New Testament Church Age runs from the start of the church in Matthew chapter ten, ending with the rapture.

There is a debate among Christians regarding the definition and manifestation of the organism called "church." Some Baptists believe in the universal and local churches. Others believe there is no universal church; only local churches. I have friends on both side of the issue. It is not a doctrine that I break fellowship over.

We must look to the Scriptures to settle the debate. Although I would be happy to believe in the "local churches only" theory, I find that to do so requires the wrestling of Scripture to fit that mold. Allow me to explain.

The word "church" is used seventy-seven times in the King James Version of the New Testament. Most of these instances speak of local congregations signified by location or context. Review these samples.

Acts 11:22

"Then tidings of these things came unto the ears of the church which was in Jerusalem: and they sent forth Barnabas, that he should go as far as Antioch."

Romans 16:1

"I commend unto you Phebe our sister, which is a servant of the church which is at Cenchrea:"

1 Corinthians 1:2

"Unto the church of God which is at Corinth, to them that are sanctified in Christ Jesus, called to be saints,

with all that in every place call upon the name of Jesus Christ our Lord, both theirs and ours:"

Colossians 4:15

"Salute the brethren which are in Laodicea, and Nymphas, and the church which is in his house."

Colossians 4:16

"And when this epistle is read among you, cause that it be read also in the church of the Laodiceans; and that ye likewise read the epistle from Laodicea."

1 Thessalonians 1:1

"Paul, and Silvanus, and Timotheus, unto the church of the Thessalonians which is in God the Father and in the Lord Jesus Christ: Grace be unto you, and peace, from God our Father, and the Lord Jesus Christ."

Some instances speak of "the church" referrring to the whole of New Testament believers. Consider these examples.

Acts 20:28

"Take heed therefore unto yourselves, and to all the flock, over the which the Holy Ghost hath made you overseers, to feed the church of God, which he hath purchased with his own blood."

1 Corinthians 12:13

"For by one Spirit are we all baptized into one body, whether we be Jews or Gentiles, whether we be bond or free; and have been all made to drink into one Spirit."

Ephesians 1:22

"And hath put all things under his feet, and gave him to be the head over all things to the church,"

Ephesians 3:21

"Unto him be glory in the church by Christ Jesus throughout all ages, world without end. Amen."

Ephesians 5:25–27

"Husbands, love your wives, even as Christ also loved the church, and gave himself for it; That he might sanctify and cleanse it with the washing of water by the word, That he might present it to himself a glorious church, not having spot, or wrinkle, or any such thing; but that it should be holy and without blemish."

Colossians 1:18

"And he is the head of the body, the church: who is the beginning, the firstborn from the dead; that in all things he might have the preeminence."

Colossians 1:24

"Who now rejoice in my sufferings for you, and fill up that which is behind of the afflictions of Christ in my flesh for his body's sake, which is the church:"

How do we rightly divide these Scriptures?

The Universal Church

Even those that don't believe in the universal church believe all Christians make up the "family of God." And for good reason. The Bible discusses all New Testament believers as a group. Many people call this concept the universal or invisible church. The Universal Church refers to all believers saved during the New Testament age.

I understand why some would attack the doctrine of the Universal Church. The concept of the universal church has been used to mislead countless souls.

The Roman Catholic Church highjacked the idea of a universal church. Catholic means "universal." They claim to be the only church and the only way to God. Their claim is heresy of the highest order. Protestant churches that came out of the Catholic church during the reformation are inclined to have a strong emphasis on the universal church. The Roman Catholic Church and the Protestant Churches that came out of it, have a long history of persecuting local churches that like ours.

Furthermore, Satan has used a corrupt idea of the Universal Church to damage Christ's local churches. Today, some professing Christians even believe that there is no need to attend a local church because they are part of an invisible church. This concept is wholly unbiblical.

The Bible does speak of all saved people as all belonging to Christ, but are they a church? The Bible says they are a church.

> *Colossians 1:24*
>
> *"Who now rejoice in my sufferings for you, and fill up that which is behind of the afflictions of Christ in my flesh for his body's sake, which is the church:"*

Yet, they are not a church in the sense that we understand today. While all believers have been "called out" of the world, they have not yet assembled.

The invisible body of Christ will become a "called out assembly" at the rapture. We refer to this as "the church in the air." Only after the rapture do we see all New Testament believers gathered as a called-out assembly.

Then we will be a Heavenly Universal Church.

> *Hebrews 12:22–23*

36

*"But ye are come unto mount Sion, and unto the city
of the living God, the heavenly Jerusalem, and to an
innumerable company of angels, To the general assembly
and church of the firstborn, which are written in heaven,
and to God the Judge of all, and to the spirits of just men
made perfect,"*

The Local Church

The word "church" comes from the Greek word "ekklesia"
which means "a called-out assembly." A New Testament
Church is a local assembly of baptized believers.

Believers should build their lives around church attendance
and ministry. As the end of days approaches, we must be
more faithful to the local church than ever before!

Hebrews 10:25

*"Not forsaking the assembling of ourselves together, as
the manner of some is; but exhorting one another: and
so much the more, as ye see the day approaching."*

Physical churches are local manifestations of the greater body
of Christ. Churches in the Bible are identified commonly by
their physical location.

Make no mistake - we promote the local church! Belief the
supernatural body of Christ does not diminish our commitment
to local churches.

God intends every Christian to operate as an active member
of a local church. Only through a local church with a pastor,
deacons, offerings, preaching, teaching, soul-winning,
ministries, etc., can we fulfill God's plan for our lives.

A local church provides a level of accountability for believers
that cannot be found anywhere else. Internet minsitries can

be a blessing, but they can never replace a local assembly of believers committed to Christ. Backsliders and carnal Christians use the concept of a "universal church" to justify their lack of commitment to the Saviour.

God describes those who must be put out of the church as "delivered to Satan." Who in their right mind would do that to themselves??

1 Corinthians 5:5

"To deliver such an one unto Satan for the destruction of the flesh, that the spirit may be saved in the day of the Lord Jesus."

Clearly, Satan has much more power to destroy God's children who are not part of a good local church.

In Scripture, we find the beautiful symphony of two important doctrines regarding Christ's churches.

The Bible explains that every believer in the church age is part of the body of Christ. The local bodies of Christ (physical churches) are manifestations of the invisible body of Christ (all believers).

A Final Thought.

There is one other passage of Scripture regarding the baptism of the Holy Ghost that we must consider - Acts 1:4-5.

Does it use the phrase baptism of the Holy Ghost for God's power?

Yes, but it doesn't stop there. It means so much more.

Here's why...

Acts 1:5

"And, being assembled together with them, commanded

them that they should not depart from Jerusalem, but wait for the promise of the Father, which, saith he, ye have heard of me. For John truly baptized with water; but ye shall be baptized with the Holy Ghost not many days hence."

Jesus Christ was the bridge between the Old and New Testaments. He fulfilled the law and set in motion the New Testament age.

The Disciples had already had the Holy Ghost breathed upon them by Christ and experienced the firstfruits of His benefits.

John 20:22

"And when he had said this, he breathed on them, and saith unto them, Receive ye the Holy Ghost:"

In Acts chapter one, the full arrival of the Holy Spirit was announced.

This would fulfill great OT prophecies like the following.

Isaiah 44:3

"For I will pour water upon him that is thirsty, And floods upon the dry ground: I will pour my spirit upon thy seed, And my blessing upon thine offspring:"

Joel 2:28–29

"And it shall come to pass afterward, That I will pour out my spirit upon all flesh; And your sons and your daughters shall prophesy, Your old men shall dream dreams, Your young men shall see visions: And also upon the servants and upon the handmaids In those days will I pour out my spirit."

The Holy Ghost began His full New Testament ministry at Pentecost. From that moment on we see Him fully engaged with the church.

In conclusion, the terms anointing, baptism, and filling of the Holy Spirit identify different doctrines.

The Baptism of the Holy Ghost is a benefit of salvation immersing us into Christ's death, burial, resurrection, and body.

5

The Indwelling Of The Holy Spirit

John 14:16–17

"And I will pray the Father, and he shall give you another Comforter, that he may abide with you for ever; [17] Even the Spirit of truth; whom the world cannot receive, because it seeth him not, neither knoweth him: but ye know him; for he dwelleth with you, and shall be in you."

Let's learn about God's amazing work within every believer through the indwelling of the Holy Spirit.

Before Jesus Christ ascended back to Heaven, He promised to leave us a Comforter to assist us. The presence of God through the Holy Spirit that dwells within us is a priceless benefit of our salvation. However, many Christians live daily without any thought of the spiritual powerhouse available within us.

When I was a young bus kid attending church sporadically,

I would hear the preacher teach about the Holy Spirit living within us. Admittedly, it sounded weird to me! I had watched too many sci-fi movies, so the idea of something living within us provided many interesting mental pictures.

I knew a family in which one young child was witnessing to her younger brother.

She asked him, "If we cut your heart open, would we find a little Jesus?" Ha! Some of these doctrines can be hard to understand.

However, God will teach us these great truths when we listen to His Word with an open heart.

I thank God for the Holy Spirit.

There should never be a day that you don't think about the amazing gift of the Holy Spirit Who lives within you.

So many well-intentioned believers lack spiritual power because they don't understand the indwelling of the Holy Spirit.

The Holy Spirit dwells within you! He opens a world of possibilities for you.

Consider three truths about the indwelling of the Holy Spirit.

1. The Indwelling of the Holy Spirit Promised.

John 14:16–17

"And I will pray the Father, and he shall give you another Comforter, that he may abide with you for ever; [17] Even the Spirit of truth; whom the world cannot receive, because it seeth him not, neither knoweth him: but ye know him; for he dwelleth with you, and shall be in you."

The indwelling of the Holy Spirit is one of the benefits of

Christ's finished work on the Cross. Before the sin debt was paid, the Holy Spirit would come upon Old Testament saints for specific tasks. However, He could not remain upon them or dwell in them.

The Spirit came upon Caleb.

Judges 3:10

"And the Spirit of the Lord came upon him, and he judged Israel, and went out to war: and the Lord delivered Chushan-rishathaim king of Mesopotamia into his hand; and his hand prevailed against Chushan-rishathaim. "

The Spirit came upon Gideon.

Judges 6:34

"But the Spirit of the Lord came upon Gideon, and he blew a trumpet; and Abi-ezer was gathered after him."

The Spirit came upon Samson.

Judges 14:5–6

"Then went Samson down, and his father and his mother, to Timnath, and came to the vineyards of Timnath: and, behold, a young lion roared against him. ⁶And the Spirit of the Lord came mightily upon him, and he rent him as he would have rent a kid, and he had nothing in his hand: but he told not his father or his mother what he had done."

The Holy Spirit gave Samson his supernatural power.

David knew that he had experienced the wisdom and power of God through the Holy Spirit, but was concerned that the Spirit would leave him because of sin.

After his sin with Bathsheba, David prayed that God would

not take the Holy Spirit from him.

Psalm 51:10–12

"Create in me a clean heart, O God; And renew a right spirit within me. [11] Cast me not away from thy presence; And take not thy holy spirit from me. [12] Restore unto me the joy of thy salvation; And uphold me with thy free spirit."

In the Old Testament, God promised that the Holy Spirit would be inside His people one day.

Ezekiel 36:27

"And I will put my spirit within you, and cause you to walk in my statutes, and ye shall keep my judgments, and do them."

What a tremendous promise!

2. The Indwelling of the Holy Spirit Proclaimed.

In the New Testament era, all believers are universally and permanently indwelt by the Holy Spirit. The promises of the Old Testament have been fulfilled!

Consider this interesting question.

Where is God right now?

I believe the answer has two important distinctions.

A. God is everywhere all the time.

He is omnipresent. He is everywhere at the same time. Find all the times in the following verses that tell us where God's presence abides.

Psalm 139:1–12

"O Lord, thou hast searched me, and known me. [2] Thou knowest my downsitting and mine uprising, Thou

44

understandest my thought afar off. ³ Thou compassest my path and my lying down, And art acquainted with all my ways. ⁴ For there is not a word in my tongue, But, lo, O Lord, thou knowest it altogether. ⁵ Thou hast beset me behind and before, And laid thine hand upon me. ⁶ Such knowledge is too wonderful for me; It is high, I cannot attain unto it. ⁷ Whither shall I go from thy spirit? Or whither shall I flee from thy presence? ⁸ If I ascend up into heaven, thou art there: If I make my bed in hell, behold, thou art there. ⁹ If I take the wings of the morning, And dwell in the uttermost parts of the sea; ¹⁰ Even there shall thy hand lead me, And thy right hand shall hold me. ¹¹ If I say, Surely the darkness shall cover me; Even the night shall be light about me. ¹² Yea, the darkness hideth not from thee; But the night shineth as the day: The darkness and the light are both alike to thee."

There is no where the Psalmist could go to escape God's presence. God is everywhere!

Since God is omnipresent, He doesn't live in temples or churches.

Acts 7:48

"Howbeit the most High dwelleth not in temples made with hands; as saith the prophet,"

Acts 17:24

"God that made the world and all things therein, seeing that he is Lord of heaven and earth, dwelleth not in temples made with hands;"

Some religions teach that certain areas or specific buildings are where the gods live.

Even though churches are sacred houses of God, our Lord does not live in them.

No building could contain God. His seat of power is in Heaven. His presence is everywhere.

B. God lives within Believers.

Yet in this age, He lives within His people in the person of the Holy Spirit.

Think of it! Almighty God chose to put a piece of Himself within us to seal us and empower us.

Where does God live? Within His people in the Person of the Holy Spirit!

How far away is God? He is within you!

Believers are permanently indwelt with the Holy Spirit. God will never leave us nor forsake us.

> *Hebrews 13:5*
>
> *"Let your conversation be without covetousness; and be content with such things as ye have: for he hath said, I will never leave thee, nor forsake thee."*

Consider seven passages of Scripture that teach us about the indwelling of the Holy Spirit.

> *Romans 8:11*
>
> *"But if the Spirit of him that raised up Jesus from the dead dwell in you, he that raised up Christ from the dead shall also quicken your mortal bodies by his Spirit that dwelleth in you."*
>
> *1 Corinthians 3:16*
>
> *"Know ye not that ye are the temple of God, and that the Spirit of God dwelleth in you?"*

2 Corinthians 1:22

"Who hath also sealed us, and given the earnest of the Spirit in our hearts."

Ephesians 1:13–14

"In whom ye also trusted, after that ye heard the word of truth, the gospel of your salvation: in whom also after that ye believed, ye were sealed with that holy Spirit of promise, ¹⁴ Which is the earnest of our inheritance until the redemption of the purchased possession, unto the praise of his glory."

2 Timothy 1:14

"That good thing which was committed unto thee keep by the Holy Ghost which dwelleth in us."

James 4:5

"Do ye think that the scripture saith in vain, The spirit that dwelleth in us lusteth to envy?"

1 John 3:24

"And he that keepeth his commandments dwelleth in him, and he in him. And hereby we know that he abideth in us, by the Spirit which he hath given us."

When was the Holy Spirit given to God's children?

Some believe the Holy Spirit was given to the disciples by Christ in John 20:22.

John 20:22

"And when he had said this, he breathed on them, and saith unto them, Receive ye the Holy Ghost:"

Others believe the Holy Spirit came to indwell believers at Pentecost. Those who believe the Spirit was given in John

20:22 assert that Holy Spirit was already indwelling believers but came in power upon the disciples at Pentecost.

Acts 2:1–4

"And when the day of Pentecost was fully come, they were all with one accord in one place. ² And suddenly there came a sound from heaven as of a rushing mighty wind, and it filled all the house where they were sitting. ³ And there appeared unto them cloven tongues like as of fire, and it sat upon each of them. ⁴ And they were all filled with the Holy Ghost, and began to speak with other tongues, as the Spirit gave them utterance."

Personally, I believe that our Lord released the Holy Ghost in John 20:22, but told the disciples to wait until He arrived in power. The Spirit came in fulness of power on Pentecost.

Luke 24:49

"And, behold, I send the promise of my Father upon you: but tarry ye in the city of Jerusalem, until ye be endued with power from on high."

Whichever position you hold, we can all agree that He is here and the Holy Ghost indwells believers!

When does the Holy Spirit move in to the believer?

At the moment you were born again through faith in Christ, you were indwelt and sealed with the Holy Spirit. Examine the Apostle Paul's interaction with this group of professing believers at Ephesus.

Acts 19:1–7

"And it came to pass, that, while Apollos was at Corinth, Paul having passed through the upper coasts came to Ephesus: and finding certain disciples, ² He said unto

them, Have ye received the Holy Ghost since ye believed? And they said unto him, We have not so much as heard whether there be any Holy Ghost. ³ And he said unto them, Unto what then were ye baptized? And they said, Unto John's baptism. ⁴ Then said Paul, John verily baptized with the baptism of repentance, saying unto the people, that they should believe on him which should come after him, that is, on Christ Jesus. ⁵ When they heard this, they were baptized in the name of the Lord Jesus. ⁶ And when Paul had laid his hands upon them, the Holy Ghost came on them; and they spake with tongues, and prophesied. ⁷ And all the men were about twelve."

These sincere people had been baptized by John the Baptist, but had not fully understood the finished work of Christ. They didn't even know the Holy Ghost existed!

After their faith was settled, they exhibited the sign gifts of the Spirit to validate their salvation.

What are sign gifts? They were special abilities or outworkings of the Holy Spirit that were given in the first days of Christianity as an outward manifestation of inward salvation.

For example, the Jews didn't believe that Gentiles could be saved until they saw the sign gifts of the Holy Spirit in them.

Acts 10:43–48

"To him give all the prophets witness, that through his name whosoever believeth in him shall receive remission of sins. ⁴⁴ While Peter yet spake these words, the Holy Ghost fell on all them which heard the word. ⁴⁵ And they of the circumcision which believed were astonished, as many as came with Peter, because that on the Gentiles also was poured out the gift of the Holy Ghost. ⁴⁶ For

they heard them speak with tongues, and magnify God. Then answered Peter, ⁴⁷ Can any man forbid water, that these should not be baptized, which have received the Holy Ghost as well as we? ⁴⁸ And he commanded them to be baptized in the name of the Lord. Then prayed they him to tarry certain days."

Also, the disciples worked special miracles in the infancy of Christianity to display God's saving power to the world. These sign gifts were no longer necessary once we received the written Word of God.

1 Corinthians 13:8–11

"Charity never faileth: but whether there be prophecies, they shall fail; whether there be tongues, they shall cease; whether there be knowledge, it shall vanish away. ⁹ For we know in part, and we prophesy in part. ¹⁰ But when that which is perfect is come, then that which is in part shall be done away. ¹¹ When I was a child, I spake as a child, I understood as a child, I thought as a child: but when I became a man, I put away childish things."

Where does the Spirit live within us?

The Bible says that the Holy Spirit resides within our bodies.

1 Corinthians 6:19–20

"What? know ye not that your body is the temple of the Holy Ghost which is in you, which ye have of God, and ye are not your own? ²⁰ For ye are bought with a price: therefore glorify God in your body, and in your spirit, which are God's."

Of course, the Holy Spirit doesn't reside in our physical flesh.

Romans 7:17–18

"Now then it is no more I that do it, but sin that dwelleth in me. [18] For I know that in me (that is, in my flesh,) dwelleth no good thing: for to will is present with me; but how to perform that which is good I find not."

Sin has corrupted our flesh. Where does the Holy Spirit live within us? The Holy Spirit lives in our resurrected spirit.

Before salvation, we are dead in trespasses and sins. The lost are literally dead men walking. When we put our faith in the death, burial, and resurrection of Christ, we are born again as our dead spirit is raised to new life in Christ!

Romans 8:8–11

"So then they that are in the flesh cannot please God. [9] But ye are not in the flesh, but in the Spirit, if so be that the Spirit of God dwell in you. Now if any man have not the Spirit of Christ, he is none of his. [10] And if Christ be in you, the body is dead because of sin; but the Spirit is life because of righteousness. [11] But if the Spirit of him that raised up Jesus from the dead dwell in you, he that raised up Christ from the dead shall also quicken your mortal bodies by his Spirit that dwelleth in you."

Ephesians 2:1

"And you hath he quickened, who were dead in trespasses and sins;"

Ephesians 2:5–9

"Even when we were dead in sins, hath quickened us together with Christ, (by grace ye are saved;) [6] And hath raised us up together, and made us sit together in heavenly places in Christ Jesus: [7] That in the ages to come he might shew the exceeding riches of his grace in his kindness toward us through Christ Jesus. [8] For by grace are ye

saved through faith; and that not of yourselves: it is the gift of God: ⁹ *Not of works, lest any man should boast."*

The Holy Spirit resides within our spirit.

Imagine a circle that represents your body. In your mind, draw a smaller circle within it that represents your soul.

Now, picture a still smaller circle within the second that represents your spirit.

Now, imagine a smaller circle within the third one that represents the Holy Spirit. The Holy Ghost lives within our born again spirit, in that part of us that cannot sin – the new man.

1 John 3:9

"Whosoever is born of God doth not commit sin; for his seed remaineth in him: and he cannot sin, because he is born of God."

The Holy Spirit dwells within our resurrected spirit. He communicates with our spirit.

Romans 8:16

"The Spirit itself beareth witness with our spirit, that we are the children of God:"

3. The Indwelling of the Holy Spirit Produces.

The Holy Spirit is the spiritual power that resides within us. In a later chapter, we will discuss the 34 activities of the Holy Spirit. For now, I will give you a few of the important works that He accomplishes in our lives.

The Spirit Seals Our Salvation.

Ephesians 1:12–14

"That we should be to the praise of his glory, who first

trusted in Christ. 13 In whom ye also trusted, after that ye heard the word of truth, the gospel of your salvation: in whom also after that ye believed, ye were sealed with that holy Spirit of promise, 14 Which is the earnest of our inheritance until the redemption of the purchased possession, unto the praise of his glory."

Don't miss this astonishing truth! God has given you the Holy Spirit as a guarantee that He will take you to Heaven someday. If He were to let you go to Hell, the Holy Spirit would have to go to Hell too!

That is impossible! Is there any greater proof of the security of the believer?

God promised to save you. Then He gave you the indwelling Holy Spirit as a pledge of Heaven to come.

The Spirit Works in us to Do God's Will.

Philippians 2:13

"For it is God which worketh in you both to will and to do of his good pleasure."

God works in us to desire His will (to will) and empowers us to accomplish it (to do).

How does He work in us? Through the Holy Spirit Who dwells within us.

Zechariah 4:6

"Then he answered and spake unto me, saying, This is the word of the Lord unto Zerubbabel, saying, Not by might, nor by power, but by my spirit, Saith the Lord of hosts."

The Spirit Connects Us To God.

The Holy Spirit is our spiritual Helper that connects us to God and empowers us to live like Him.

John 14:16

"And I will pray the Father, and he shall give you another Comforter, that he may abide with you for ever;"

The word "another" in this verse means "another of the same kind." Since Christ was leaving Earth to return to Heaven, He left the Holy Spirit in His place.

John 14:18

"I will not leave you comfortless: I will come to you."

Jesus explained that it was better for Him to go and leave us the Holy Spirit.

John 16:7

"Nevertheless I tell you the truth; It is expedient for you that I go away: for if I go not away, the Comforter will not come unto you; but if I depart, I will send him unto you."

Through the Spirit, Christ can indwell and empower all of us at the same time.

The Godhead (Father, Son, and Holy Spirit) is co-equal. If you have one, you have access to the others. The Spirit is Christ in us.

Colossians 1:27

"To whom God would make known what is the riches of the glory of this mystery among the Gentiles; which is Christ in you, the hope of glory:"

Because of the indwelling Holy Spirit we can say Christ lives in us.

Galatians 2:20

"I am crucified with Christ: nevertheless I live; yet not I, but Christ liveth in me: and the life which I now live in the flesh I live by the faith of the Son of God, who loved me, and gave himself for me."

The indwelling Holy Spirit was promised to God's people in the Old Testament.

That promise was fulfilled after the death, burial, and resurrection of Jesus Christ.

Today, the Holy Spirit universally and permanently indwells every believer. He is Christ in us, the hope of glory, and the spiritual power that enables us to live like Christ accomplishing the will of God.

Thank God for the indwelling Holy Spirit!

Never let a day go by that you don't praise God for His indwelling Spirit.

Yield to God each day asking to be filled with His Spirit.

6

The Seal Of
The Holy Spirit

Ephesians 1:12–14

*"That we should be to the praise of his glory, who first
trusted in Christ. In whom ye also trusted, after that ye
heard the word of truth, the gospel of your salvation: in
whom also after that ye believed, ye were sealed with
that holy Spirit of promise, Which is the earnest of
our inheritance until the redemption of the purchased
possession, unto the praise of his glory."*

The seal of the Spirit is an exciting doctrine with tremendous
benefits for the believer.

What does it mean to be sealed with the Spirit? The seal held
significant meaning for people during Bible times. A seal could
be anything from wax impressed with a signet ring to stone
etched with an emblem. One would put his seal on items for
several important reasons.

Let's examine the multifaceted meaning of the symbol of the seal as it relates to the seal of the Spirit.

1. Seal of Authenticity.

People would give their personal seal (stamp or signature) to certify authenticity, much like a signature functions today.

John 3:33

"He that hath received his testimony hath set to his seal that God is true."

This little-known verse explains that when people accept Christ, they are "signing their name" to the fact that God is true.

God sealed us with the Holy Spirit to authenticate our salvation. The incredible gift of Himself to each believer confirms their salvation.

Those sealed with the Spirit are true believers reserved for Heaven.

Romans 8:9

"But ye are not in the flesh, but in the Spirit, if so be that the Spirit of God dwell in you. Now if any man have not the Spirit of Christ, he is none of his."

If you are not sealed by the Holy Spirit, you are not saved. If you have the Spirit dwelling in you then your salvation is authentic!

2. The Seal of Ownership.

A seal was used to show ownership. If something carried your seal, it was an announcement to all that you owned it. A seal expressed the legal right of possession.

We are sealed with the Spirit proving that we belong to God.

1 Corinthians 6:18–20

"Flee fornication. Every sin that a man doeth is without the body; but he that committeth fornication sinneth against his own body. [19] What? know ye not that your body is the temple of the Holy Ghost which is in you, which ye have of God, and ye are not your own? [20] For ye are bought with a price: therefore glorify God in your body, and in your spirit, which are God's."

Christ purchased our body, soul, and spirit on Calvary. We belong to Him!

3. The Seal of Authority.

A seal was employed to express authority.

For example, an edict from the king would be inscribed with the royal seal. In addition, royal servants could wear the seal of the king. Everyone was expected to listen to the emissary as if the King was speaking.

Christians operate as God's representatives in the world. The seal of the Holy Spirit gives us divine authority to accomplish the work of God.

2 Corinthians 5:20–21

"Now then we are ambassadors for Christ, as though God did beseech you by us: we pray you in Christ's stead, be ye reconciled to God.

For he hath made him to be sin for us, who knew no sin; that we might be made the righteousness of God in him."

We remain in this world in the place of Christ. He directed us to continue His work. We have a divine commission to continue Christ's mission and the authority to do so.

John 20:21

"Then said Jesus to them again, Peace be unto you: as my Father hath sent me, even so send I you."

4. The Seal of Security.

A seal provided security. People knew the item hadn't been tampered with if the seal was unbroken.

Many years ago, the process of canning food changed how long perishable food could be stored. By placing food in a jar and creating a seal with a lid, corruption could not enter. Food would not spoil because it was protected by a seal.

This concept is easily understood if you think about the many jars of food in the supermarket. Consider a jar of pickles. (Who doesn't like pickles? Never trust someone who doesn't like pickles. Lol.) There is a button on the lid that ensures the seal hasn't been broken. When you open the lid there is a pop that signals the seal has been breached. If the seal is broken, the food is spoiled.

We have been sealed by the Spirit as divine protection!

The seal of God was demonstrated in the life of Job. Satan could not touch Job without God's permission.

Job 1:9–12

"Then Satan answered the LORD, and said, Doth Job fear God for nought? Hast not thou made an hedge about him, and about his house, and about all that he hath on every side? thou hast blessed the work of his hands, and his substance is increased in the land. But put forth thine hand now, and touch all that he hath, and he will curse thee to thy face. And the LORD said unto Satan, Behold, all that he hath is in thy power; only upon himself put not

forth thine hand. So Satan went forth from the presence
of the LORD."

Also, the seal of security is shown in the future in the book of
the Revelation.

Revelation 9:4

*"And it was commanded them that they should not hurt
the grass of the earth, neither any green thing, neither
any tree; but only those men which have not the seal of
God in their foreheads."*

Believers are protected from Satan and his minions. We have
the seal of God!

5. The Seal of Assurance.

The indwelling of the Holy Spirit is a guarantee that God will
fulfill His commitment to take believers to Heaven.

We are saved the moment we believe the Gospel, accepting
Christ as our Saviour. This is the doctrine of salvation.

We are continually sanctified as we become more like Him in
this life. This is the doctrine of sanctification.

One day we will be glorified as we leave this world to enter
Heaven. At that moment, our salvation will be complete! This
is the doctrine of glorification.

The indwelling Holy Spirit is called the earnest of the Spirit.

2 Corinthians 1:22

*"Who hath also sealed us, and given the earnest of the
Spirit in our hearts."*

God uses the same phrase in 2 Corinthians 5:5.

2 Corinthians 5:5

"Now he that hath wrought us for the selfsame thing

is God, who also hath given unto us the earnest of the Spirit."

What is an earnest? It is an advance on what is to come. It is the first payment or deposit that promises full payment in the future.

When you buy property, there is earnest money, or a down payment, required to prove your intention to follow through with the transaction. If the buyer backs out of the deal, he forfeits the earnest money.

The seal of the Holy Spirit is the assurance that God will keep His Word and take believers to Heaven.

The indwelling Spirit is called the firstfruits.

The firstfruits were the very first of the harvest to become ripe. The rest of the harvest was sure to follow but needed more time to mature.

The Holy Spirit is the first benefit of our eternal salvation! The rest is sure to come!

Ephesians 1:13–14

"In whom ye also trusted, after that ye heard the word of truth, the gospel of your salvation: in whom also after that ye believed, ye were sealed with that holy Spirit of promise, Which is the earnest of our inheritance until the redemption of the purchased possession, unto the praise of his glory."

Ephesians 4:30

"And grieve not the holy Spirit of God, whereby ye are sealed unto the day of redemption."

We are the purchased possession. The day of redemption is the day we go to Heaven. The seal of the Spirit is God's guarantee.

Don't miss this astonishing truth! God has given you the Holy Spirit as a guarantee that He will take you to Heaven someday. If He were to let you go to Hell, the Holy Spirit would have to go to Hell too! That is impossible! Is there any greater proof of the security of the believer?

God promised to save you. Then He gave you the indwelling Holy Spirit as a pledge of Heaven to come. Thanks be to God for the earnest of the Spirit!

The seal of the Holy Spirit is an extraordinary gift.

It proves:

1. Authenticity of our Salvation

2. Ownership of our Salvation

3. Authority of our Salvation

4. Security of our Salvation

5. Assurance of our Salvation

Praise God for the seal of the Holy Spirit.

7

Anointed With The Holy Spirit

Some Christians use the terms anointing, baptism, and filling of the Holy Spirit interchangeably. The Bible teaches that they are different. Each of these doctrines have important theological implications.

Let's investigate and learn what it means to be anointed with the Holy Spirit.

Our Lord Jesus Christ was anointed with the Holy Spirit.

Isaiah 61:1

"The Spirit of the Lord GOD is upon me; Because the LORD hath anointed me to preach good tidings unto the meek; He hath sent me to bind up the brokenhearted, To proclaim liberty to the captives, And the opening of the prison to them that are bound;"

New Testament saints are anointed with the Holy Spirit.

1 John 2:20

"But ye have an unction from the Holy One, and ye know all things."

The word "unction" is the same Greek word as "anointing" in verse 27.

1 John 2:27

"But the anointing which ye have received of him abideth in you, and ye need not that any man teach you: but as the same anointing teacheth you of all things, and is truth, and is no lie, and even as it hath taught you, ye shall abide in him."

Consider the context of these verses. The Apostle John was warning these believers that there are many antichrists and enemies of God. However, he had confidence in them because they had the unction or anointing of the Holy Spirit.

1 John 2:18–20

"Little children, it is the last time: and as ye have heard that antichrist shall come, even now are there many antichrists; whereby we know that it is the last time. [19] *They went out from us, but they were not of us; for if they had been of us, they would no doubt have continued with us: but they went out, that they might be made manifest that they were not all of us.* [20] *But ye have an unction from the Holy One, and ye know all things."*

Only those who have the Holy Spirit are truly born again.

1 John 3:24

"And he that keepeth his commandments dwelleth in him, and he in him. And hereby we know that he abideth in us, by the Spirit which he hath given us."

I believe this anointing in 1 John chapter two speaks of being sealed with the Holy Spirit at the moment of salvation.

As we have already discussed, Ephesians chapter one speaks of this concept as well.

> *Ephesians 1:12–14*
>
> *"That we should be to the praise of his glory, who first trusted in Christ. [13] In whom ye also trusted, after that ye heard the word of truth, the gospel of your salvation: in whom also after that ye believed, ye were sealed with that holy Spirit of promise, [14] Which is the earnest of our inheritance until the redemption of the purchased possession, unto the praise of his glory."*

What is an anointing?

Webster's 1828 dictionary defines the noun form of the word anointing as "the active smearing with oil; a consecrating." How would one be anointed with the Spirit?

Let's examine what the Bible says about anointing to gain some insight.

1. Purpose Of Anointing In Scripture.

Oil has been used throughout history for many uses. Some soldiers would rub their shields with oil. Many cultures would use oil for cosmetic or healing purposes.

The Bible is full of diverse examples of sacred anointing, but they all had one thing in common. In the spiritual ritual, anointing oil was used for consecration. An anointed object was sanctified, or set apart, for God. It was no longer considered common.

Special ingredients were added to the oil symbolizing the Holy Spirit. Anointing with this oil was a physical recognition of their particular role or duty in the sight of God. It was a recognition of the Lord's divine calling upon their lives.

2. Examples Of Anointing In Scripture.

1. An Old Testament priest's clothing was anointed.

Exodus 28:40–41

"And for Aaron's sons thou shalt make coats, and thou shalt make for them girdles, and bonnets shalt thou make for them, for glory and for beauty. [41] *And thou shalt put them upon Aaron thy brother, and his sons with him; and shalt anoint them, and consecrate them, and sanctify them, that they may minister unto me in the priest's office."*

2. Furniture of the tabernacle and temple were anointed with this sacred oil.

Exodus 30:22–29

"Moreover the LORD spake unto Moses, saying, [23] *Take thou also unto thee principal spices, of pure myrrh five hundred shekels, and of sweet cinnamon half so much, even two hundred and fifty shekels, and of sweet calamus two hundred and fifty shekels,* [24] *And of cassia five hundred shekels, after the shekel of the sanctuary, and of oil olive an hin:* [25] *And thou shalt make it an oil of holy ointment, an ointment compound after the art of the apothecary: it shall be an holy anointing oil.* [26] *And thou shalt anoint the tabernacle of the congregation therewith, and the ark of the testimony,* [27] *And the table and all his vessels, and the candlestick and his vessels, and the altar of incense,* [28] *And the altar of burnt offering with all his vessels, and the laver and his foot.* [29] *And thou shalt sanctify them, that they may be most holy: whatsoever toucheth them shall be holy."*

3. The priests themselves were anointed and consecrated to God.

Exodus 30:30

"And thou shalt anoint Aaron and his sons, and consecrate them, that they may minister unto me in the priest's office."

4. The sacred formulation of oil was not to be used for any common cause. It was reserved for God alone.

Exodus 30:31–33

"And thou shalt speak unto the children of Israel, saying, This shall be an holy anointing oil unto me throughout your generations. ³² Upon man's flesh shall it not be poured, neither shall ye make any other like it, after the composition of it: it is holy, and it shall be holy unto you. ³³ Whosoever compoundeth any like it, or whosoever putteth any of it upon a stranger, shall even be cut off from his people."

5. Also, a sacred perfume was created for holy purposes. Once again, it was not to be used for any other purpose.

Exodus 30:34–38

"And the LORD said unto Moses, Take unto thee sweet spices, stacte, and onycha, and galbanum; these sweet spices with pure frankincense: of each shall there be a like weight: ³⁵ And thou shalt make it a perfume, a confection after the art of the apothecary, tempered together, pure and holy: ³⁶ And thou shalt beat some of it very small, and put of it before the testimony in the tabernacle of the congregation, where I will meet with thee: it shall be unto you most holy. ³⁷ And as for the perfume which thou shalt make, ye shall not make to yourselves according to

the composition thereof: it shall be unto thee holy for the LORD. [38] *Whosoever shall make like unto that, to smell thereto, shall even be cut off from his people."*

6. Priests were anointed.

Exodus 40:13–15

"And thou shalt put upon Aaron the holy garments, and anoint him, and sanctify him; that he may minister unto me in the priest's office. [14] *And thou shalt bring his sons, and clothe them with coats:* [15] *And thou shalt anoint them, as thou didst anoint their father, that they may minister unto me in the priest's office: for their anointing shall surely be an everlasting priesthood throughout their generations."*

7. Prophets were anointed.

1 Kings 19:16

"And Jehu the son of Nimshi shalt thou anoint to be king over Israel: and Elisha the son of Shaphat of Abel-meholah shalt thou anoint to be prophet in thy room."

8. Kings were anointed.

1 Kings 1:34

"And let Zadok the priest and Nathan the prophet anoint him there king over Israel: and blow ye with the trumpet, and say, God save king Solomon."

Anointing is serious business with God. Remember that the physical act of anointing symbolizes the unseen spiritual anointing of God Himself.

God's anointed are protected.

Psalm 105:15

"Saying, Touch not mine anointed, And do my prophets no harm."

70

They are not to be injured or insulted but treated with the upmost respect.

1 Samuel 24:6

"And he said unto his men, The LORD forbid that I should do this thing unto my master, the LORD's anointed, to stretch forth mine hand against him, seeing he is the anointed of the LORD."

1 Samuel 26:9

"And David said to Abishai, Destroy him not: for who can stretch forth his hand against the LORD's anointed, and be guiltless?"

9. Medicinal oils were used for healing wounds.

Luke 10:34

"And went to him, and bound up his wounds, pouring in oil and wine, and set him on his own beast, and brought him to an inn, and took care of him."

10. Anointing oils were used to cure the sick and symbolize God's special healing for the sick during prayer.

James 5:14

"Is any sick among you? let him call for the elders of the church; and let them pray over him, anointing him with oil in the name of the Lord:"

11. Loved ones were anointed with oil in preparation for burial.

Matthew 26:12

"For in that she hath poured this ointment on my body, she did it for my burial."

3. Applications of Anointing

The beneficial use of oil has a long record throughout human history. However, the use of sacred anointing to symbolize the unseen spiritual anointing of the Holy Spirit as it is recorded in Scripture rises above the rest.

Anointing of the Spirit consecrates a person, place, or thing, for God's special use. A building can be consecrated as a church. A wooden stand can be consecrated as a pulpit. A man can be consecrated as a preacher. A Christian can be consecrated for spiritual service.

Here are a few important truths regarding the anointing of the Holy Spirit.

1. God anoints His children with the Holy Spirit at the moment of salvation.

2. An anointing signifies that you are set apart for a special purpose.

3. An anointing increases authority or capacity to accomplish more for God.

4. We can pray for a fresh anointing when our situation changes.

    a. The preacher can pray for fresh oil when he becomes a pastor.

    b. A pastor can pray for a fresh anointing when the church grows.

    c. A Christian can pray for an anointing when he becomes a Sunday school teacher, children's church worker, bus captain, soul winner, etc.

    d. Any new level is an opportunity to pray for fresh oil.

e. A parent can pray for fresh oil with each new child.

f. A parent can pray for a fresh anointing when the children reach a new stage of life.

g. A believer can pray for fresh oil when met with a new trial, burden, or life circumstance.

h. A Christian can pray for a special anointing for any new task or responsibility.

The baptism of the Holy Spirit occurs at salvation. It only happens one time.

The filling of the Holy Spirit happens as we yield to him. It is a recurring event over our lifetime.

The anointing of the Holy Spirit sanctifies us for God's special use. It can take place any time or as the situation changes.

Now that we understand the anointing of the Holy Spirit, we can rest in it to accomplish the tasks God called us to do. Also, we can pray for a fresh anointing any time our situation changes and we need more help from God.

Thank God for the anointing of the Holy Spirit.

8

Activity Of The Spirit BEFORE Salvation

God the Father, God the Son, and God the Holy Ghost each play a role in our salvation. In this chapter, we will learn the activities of the Holy Spirit that brought us to faith in Christ.

The Holy Spirit is the least understood member of the Godhead. That fact is a tragedy. It explains a major reason why modern Christianity is so weak and anemic.

The Holy Spirit was given to New Testament believers to empower them to serve Christ in this present evil world. If you are not filled with the Spirit, you are missing out on supernatural power and blessing.

Before we learn from the Scriptures about how the Holy Spirit works in the life of a believer, let's investigate what role He plays in our salvation.

A lot happens behind the scenes when a soul is saved. Consider the role of each member of the Trinity in Salvation. We won't take the time in this section for an exhaustive study. However, let's learn a few truths as we dive into the Holy Spirit's role in salvation.

1. The Father Selects Us.

Ephesians 1:3–5

"Blessed be the God and Father of our Lord Jesus Christ, who hath blessed us with all spiritual blessings in heavenly places in Christ: ⁴ According as he hath chosen us in him before the foundation of the world, that we should be holy and without blame before him in love: ⁵ Having predestinated us unto the adoption of children by Jesus Christ to himself, according to the good pleasure of his will,"

2. The Son Saves Us.

Ephesians 1:6–7

"To the praise of the glory of his grace, wherein he hath made us accepted in the beloved. ⁷ In whom we have redemption through his blood, the forgiveness of sins, according to the riches of his grace;"

3. The Spirit Seals Us.

Ephesians 1:13–14

"In whom ye also trusted, after that ye heard the word of truth, the gospel of your salvation: in whom also after that ye believed, ye were sealed with that holy Spirit of promise, ¹⁴ Which is the earnest of our inheritance until the redemption of the purchased possession, unto the praise of his glory."

Here is another way to describe the work of the Trinity in salvation.

A. Salvation was PLANNED by the Father.

Acts 2:23

"Him, being delivered by the determinate counsel and foreknowledge of God, ye have taken, and by wicked hands have crucified and slain:"

B. Salvation was PROCURED by the Son.

Acts 2:36–38

"Therefore let all the house of Israel know assuredly, that God hath made that same Jesus, whom ye have crucified, both Lord and Christ. 37 Now when they heard this, they were pricked in their heart, and said unto Peter and to the rest of the apostles, Men and brethren, what shall we do? 38 Then Peter said unto them, Repent, and be baptized every one of you in the name of Jesus Christ for the remission of sins, and ye shall receive the gift of the Holy Ghost."

C. Salvation was PERFECTED by the Spirit.

2 Corinthians 3:18

"But we all, with open face beholding as in a glass the glory of the Lord, are changed into the same image from glory to glory, even as by the Spirit of the Lord."

Clearly, each Member of the Godhead played a role in our salvation. For the purposes of this chapter, we will consider the work of the Holy Ghost that brought us to the moment of redemption.

The Activity of the Holy Spirit Before Salvation.

The Holy Spirit works in the world to bring people to Christ. Unless the Spirit of God is involved, there can be no salvation of sinners. As you read the following truths, look back at your own salvation experience to identify how the Holy Ghost worked in your life to bring you to Christ. If you are not born again, the Spirit is working to bring you to Christ right now.

1. The Holy Spirit Invites Us.

Revelation 22:17

"And the Spirit and the bride say, Come. And let him that heareth say, Come. And let him that is athirst come. And whosoever will, let him take the water of life freely."

In this fascinating portion of Scripture, we see the last invitation to salvation in the Bible. Notice the two entities calling people to Christ - the Spirit and the bride. The bride is the church, the body of Christ. The people of God were given the responsibility to proclaim the Gospel of Christ.

Mark 16:15

"And he said unto them, Go ye into all the world, and preach the gospel to every creature."

Through personal soul winning, believers must explain salvation to the lost and invite them to accept Christ as their Saviour. If we fail to invite people to Christ, we fail in our holy responsibility.

1 Corinthians 15:34

"Awake to righteousness, and sin not; for some have not the knowledge of God: I speak this to your shame."

Notice the first person mentioned in this Scripture is the Spirit. The Holy Spirit invites people to Christ, and then the bride speaks. If the Spirit does not invite first, then the bride has no power. The Spirit speaks to the heart while the bride speaks to the ears.

78

2. The Holy Spirit Draws Us.

Our Lord told us that no one could come to Him unless the Father drew him. The Father uses the Holy Spirit to invite men to salvation and draw sinners to the Saviour.

John 6:44

"No man can come to me, except the Father which hath sent me draw him: and I will raise him up at the last day."

The Father uses the Holy Spirit to draw sinners to Christ.

The word "draw" in this verse literally means "to drag." It is the same word used to describe a fisherman pulling in a net full of fish.

John 21:11

"Simon Peter went up, and drew the net to land full of great fishes, an hundred and fifty and three: and for all there were so many, yet was not the net broken."

Also, it is the same word used in John 12:32.

John 12:32

"And I, if I be lifted up from the earth, will draw all men unto me."

The Father draws sinners. Christ draws sinners. Both use the Holy Spirit as the magnet to draw people to redemption. Salvation is a miracle that can only be accomplished when the Holy Spirit draws sinners to Christ.

God draws sinners with questions as the Holy Ghost provides the answers.

There is an unseen battle in the hearts and minds of the lost before they come to Christ. Hearts burdened with sin, pain, loneliness, and regret search for solace. Minds filled with images and questions seek for peace.

- Why am I here?
- Why am I so lonely?
- Why did that happen?
- How can I go on?
- Is there a God?
- Is there a Heaven and a Hell?
- Will I go to Heaven or Hell?
- What will happen to me when I die?

Man has many questions, but Christ can answer them all!

Matthew 22:46

"And no man was able to answer him a word, neither durst any man from that day forth ask him any more questions."

Never underestimate the power of the Lord to work in the hearts of sinners. You may not see it on the outside, yet there can be a war waging on the inside. God draws sinners with questions as the Holy Ghost points them to God for the answers.

God draws sinners with love.

Everyone is looking for true love. The problem is that they don't know how to define it, and they look in all the wrong places. After hurtful friendships and failed relationships, some begin to wonder if they will ever find love. But there is a whisper in their heart telling them that real love exists if they could only find it. Enter the Holy Spirit.

The Spirit points people to Christ with an emphasis on His supernatural love.

Jeremiah 31:3

"The LORD hath appeared of old unto me, saying, Yea, I have loved thee with an everlasting love: Therefore with lovingkindness have I drawn thee."

Hosea 11:3–4

"I taught Ephraim also to go, taking them by their arms; But they knew not that I healed them. ⁴ I drew them with cords of a man, with bands of love: And I was to them as they that take off the yoke on their jaws, And I laid meat unto them."

There is no love like God's love. There is no sacrifice like the sacrifice of Christ! The Cross demonstrates the miraculous love of Christ.

Romans 5:8

"But God commendeth his love toward us, in that, while we were yet sinners, Christ died for us."

God draws sinners with love as the Holy Ghost reveals it to them through the Gospel of Christ.

3. The Holy Spirit Convicts Us.

John 16:7–11

"Nevertheless I tell you the truth; It is expedient for you that I go away: for if I go not away, the Comforter will not come unto you; but if I depart, I will send him unto you. ⁸ And when he is come, he will reprove the world of sin, and of righteousness, and of judgment: ⁹ Of sin, because they believe not on me; ¹⁰ Of righteousness, because I go to my Father, and ye see me no more; ¹¹ Of judgment, because the prince of this world is judged."

One of the Holy Spirit's roles prior to salvation is to convict us of sin, righteousness, and judgment.

Webster's 1828 Dictionary gives this definition for the word "convict."

> *1. To determine the truth of a charge against one; to prove or find guilty of a crime charged; to determine or decide to be guilty, as by the verdict of a jury, by confession, or other legal decision. The jury convicted the prisoner of a felony.*

> *2. To convince of sin; to prove or determine to be guilty, as by the conscience.*

> *They who heard it, being convicted by their own conscience, went out one by one. John 8.*

> *3. To confute; to prove or show to be false. Obs.   Brown.*

> *4. To show by proof or evidence. Obs.*

The Holy Ghost proves our guilt before God. He convinces sinners of their sin, the righteousness of Christ, and the judgment to come.

If there is no conviction there can be no conversion. Conviction is the act of convincing or compelling one to admit the truth of a charge. The conviction of the Holy Spirit is the spiritual, inner pressure to agree with God.

Conviction of sin.

We are all sinners. We are sinners by birth and by choice. We sin because we love it. We need a miracle to deliver us from sin.

Romans 3:10

"As it is written, There is none righteous, no, not one:"

Romans 3:23

"For all have sinned, and come short of the glory of God;"

Ezekiel 18:20

"The soul that sinneth, it shall die. The son shall not bear the iniquity of the father, neither shall the father bear the iniquity of the son: the righteousness of the righteous shall be upon him, and the wickedness of the wicked shall be upon him."

Conviction of Righteousness.

Jesus Christ is righteous. He is the sinless Son of God Who came to Earth to save us from our sin. He died on the Cross to pay for our sin, was buried, and rose again from the dead. He ascended back to Heaven to rule and reign. He is the only One who can save us from our sin.

2 Corinthians 5:21

"For he hath made him to be sin for us, who knew no sin; that we might be made the righteousness of God in him."

1 Timothy 2:4–6

"Who will have all men to be saved, and to come unto the knowledge of the truth. ⁵ For there is one God, and one mediator between God and men, the man Christ Jesus; ⁶ Who gave himself a ransom for all, to be testified in due time."

Conviction of Judgment.

Christ is righteous. We are sinners. The Holy Spirit convinces sinners that judgment is coming and the verdict is guilty. If we die in our sin, we cannot go to Heaven. Faith in the finished work of Christ is our only hope of salvation from eternal damnation.

John 8:24

"I said therefore unto you, that ye shall die in your sins:

for if ye believe not that I am he, ye shall die in your sins."

Revelation 21:8

"But the fearful, and unbelieving, and the abominable, and murderers, and whoremongers, and sorcerers, and idolaters, and all liars, shall have their part in the lake which burneth with fire and brimstone: which is the second death."

Hebrews 9:27

"And as it is appointed unto men once to die, but after this the judgment:"

It is the Holy Spirit that works in the heart of man to agree with Scripture in these areas.

Today is the day of salvation.

Sinners can only come to God when the Holy Spirit is working. Thankfully, God invites, draws, and convicts "all men." God wants everyone to go to Heaven.

2 Peter 3:9

"The Lord is not slack concerning his promise, as some men count slackness; but is longsuffering to us-ward, not willing that any should perish, but that all should come to repentance."

However, the Bible is clear that salvation is more than a logical choice. It is an act of personal faith in response to the Spirit's wooing. If God is inviting you to salvation today, don't delay. Today is the day of salvation. If you wait too long, you may resist the Spirit for the last time and lose the desire to be saved at all. Don't delay. Trust Christ today!

Hebrews 3:15–19

"While it is said, To day if ye will hear his voice, harden not your hearts, as in the provocation. ¹⁶For some, when they had heard, did provoke: howbeit not all that came out of Egypt by Moses. ¹⁷But with whom was he grieved forty years? was it not with them that had sinned, whose carcases fell in the wilderness? ¹⁸And to whom sware he that they should not enter into his rest, but to them that believed not? ¹⁹So we see that they could not enter in because of unbelief."

Unbelief is the sin that keeps sinners from Heaven. We must urgently remind unbelievers that today is the day of salvation.

The Holy Spirit is active before the moment of salvation, inviting, drawing, and convicting us.

Without the work of the Holy Spirit, we could not be saved. The same Spirit is tasked with helping us overcome the flesh to live like Christ. Let's live in the Spirit today.

9

Activity Of The Holy Spirit DURING Salvation

In a previous chapter we learned the three activities of the Holy Spirit "before" we get saved. In this chapter, we will investigate the Spirit's activities during salvation.

1. The Holy Spirit Births Us.

John 3:6–7

"That which is born of the flesh is flesh; and that which is born of the Spirit is spirit. [7] Marvel not that I said unto thee, Ye must be born again."

Our Lord Jesus Christ explained that no one could go to Heaven unless they are born again by the Spirit of God. Why?

Man was created as a triune being with a body, soul, and spirit. When Adam and Eve sinned in the Garden of Eden their spirits died.

Our spirit is the part of us that communicates with God. When man sinned, their connection to God was broken.

The sin nature, along with a dead spirit, is passed on to everyone born from Adam.

Romans 5:12

"Wherefore, as by one man sin entered into the world, and death by sin; and so death passed upon all men, for that all have sinned:"

Sinners are dead in trespasses and sins. Clearly, their bodies and souls are alive, but their spirits are dead.

When we accept Christ as our Saviour and believe in His finished work in our hearts, we are born again spiritually as our spirits are resurrected.

Ephesians 2:1

"And you hath he quickened, who were dead in trespasses and sins;"

The Holy Spirit births us into the family of God at the moment of salvation!

2. The Holy Spirit Quickens Us.

Romans 8:11

"But if the Spirit of him that raised up Jesus from the dead dwell in you, he that raised up Christ from the dead shall also quicken your mortal bodies by his Spirit that dwelleth in you."

At the moment of salvation, the Holy Spirit resurrected our dead spirit. We were dead in our trespasses and sins, but thanks be to God, now we are alive in Christ.

Ephesians 2:1

"And you hath he quickened, who were dead in trespasses and sins;"

Even though this sin-cursed body will die, the same power that raised Christ from the dead will resurrect and transform our bodies at the Rapture.

Those saints who are still living when the Rapture happens will have their bodies transformed into glorified, spiritual bodies in the twinkling of an eye.

1 Corinthians 15:50–53

"Now this I say, brethren, that flesh and blood cannot inherit the kingdom of God; neither doth corruption inherit incorruption. ⁵¹ Behold, I shew you a mystery; We shall not all sleep, but we shall all be changed, ⁵² In a moment, in the twinkling of an eye, at the last trump: for the trumpet shall sound, and the dead shall be raised incorruptible, and we shall be changed. ⁵³ For this corruptible must put on incorruption, and this mortal must put on immortality."

Those saints who are in Heaven during the Rapture will shed their temporary glorified bodies to be given their eternal glorified body at theRrapture.

1 Thessalonians 4:13–18

"But I would not have you to be ignorant, brethren, concerning them which are asleep, that ye sorrow not, even as others which have no hope. ¹⁴ For if we believe that Jesus died and rose again, even so them also which sleep in Jesus will God bring with him. ¹⁵ For this we say unto you by the word of the Lord, that we which are alive and remain unto the coming of the Lord shall not

prevent them which are asleep. [16] For the Lord himself shall descend from heaven with a shout, with the voice of the archangel, and with the trump of God: and the dead in Christ shall rise first: [17] Then we which are alive and remain shall be caught up together with them in the clouds, to meet the Lord in the air: and so shall we ever be with the Lord. [18] Wherefore comfort one another with these words."

3. The Holy Spirit Adopts Us.

Romans 8:15

"For ye have not received the spirit of bondage again to fear; but ye have received the Spirit of adoption, whereby we cry, Abba, Father."

Believers are two-fold the children of God.

Once through the NEW BIRTH. This speaks of the undeniable bond of a biological connection.

Second through the ADOPTION. This speaks of God's choice. He decided to pick you. He knew what He was getting into when He adopted you.

Conception and Adoption are not competing truths. They work together showing multiple dimensions of our glorious salvation.

The illustration of adoption in the New Testament has its root in Roman law.

Jews didn't have a law for adoption. If a man died, his brother would automatically become the head of his household. There was no need for the concept of adoption in Jewish society.

However, adoption had a powerful meaning in Roman culture.

1. The adoptive parents freely chose the adopted child

ensuring they were desired by the parents.

2. The adopted child received a new identity.

3. Any prior commitments, responsibilities, or debts of the adopted child were erased.

4. An adopted child could not be disowned by the adoptive parents. Through adoption, these children became a permanent part of the family.

The Holy Spirit adopts us into the family of God at the moment of salvation. We are eternally secure in this "so great salvation."

4. The Holy Spirit Baptizes Us.

The word baptize means to immerse. For example, believers are baptized in water after salvation to act out the faith in their heart. They are immersed in the water to symbolize their faith in the death, burial, and resurrection. This is a visible symbol of faith and and important act of obedience showing a new believer's desire to follow the Saviour.

There is an unseen baptism that occurs during salvation.

1 Corinthians 12:13

"For by one Spirit are we all baptized into one body, whether we be Jews or Gentiles, whether we be bond or free; and have been all made to drink into one Spirit."

At the moment of salvation we are baptized or immersed into the body of Christ. We become a part of that great throng of multitudes that believe on Christ for salvation.

Colossians 1:24

"Who now rejoice in my sufferings for you, and fill up that which is behind of the afflictions of Christ in my

flesh for his body's sake, which is the church:"

Thankfully, our Lord gives us local churches that are assemblies of born-again, baptized believers in our communities.

God speaks about His people as a group occasionally, but provided local assembly to help them remain faithful unto the Saviour.

Consider why it is important to be faithful to Church.

Hebrews 10:23-25

"Let us hold fast the profession of our faith without wavering; (for he is faithful that promised;) 24 And let us consider one another to provoke unto love and to good works: 25 Not forsaking the assembling of ourselves together, as the manner of some is; but exhorting one another: and so much the more, as ye see the day approaching."

If we hope to hold fast our profession without wavering, we need a group of Christians in our community to provoke us to love and good works. We don't need less church in these last days. We need more church!

At the moment of salvation, the Holy Spirit baptizes us into the body of Christ.

5. The Holy Spirit Indwells Us.

John 14:17

"Even the Spirit of truth; whom the world cannot receive, because it seeth him not, neither knoweth him: but ye know him; for he dwelleth with you, and shall be in you."

In the New Testament era, all believers are universally and permanently indwelt by the Holy Spirit.

No building could contain God. His seat of power is in Heaven. His presence is everywhere.

Yet in this age, He lives within His people in the person of the Holy Spirit.

Think of it! Almighty God chose to put a piece of Himself within us to seal us and empower us.

Where does God live? Within His people in the person of the Holy Spirit! How far away is God? He is within you!

Believers are permanently indwelt with the Holy Spirit. God will never leave us nor forsake us.

Hebrews 13:5

"Let your conversation be without covetousness; and be content with such things as ye have: for he hath said, I will never leave thee, nor forsake thee."

The indwelling Holy Spirit was promised to God's people in the Old Testament.

That promise was fulfilled after the death, burial, and resurrection of Jesus Christ.

Today, the Holy Spirit universally and permanently indwells every believer. He is Christ in us, the hope of glory, and the spiritual power that enables us to live like Christ accomplishing the will of God.

6. The Holy Spirit Seals Us.

Not only does the Holy Spirit indwell us, but also, He seals us.

Ephesians 1:13

"In whom ye also trusted, after that ye heard the word of truth, the gospel of your salvation: in whom also after that ye believed, ye were sealed with that holy Spirit of promise,"

The seal of the Spirit is an exciting doctrine with tremendous benefits for the believer.

What does it mean to be sealed with the Spirit?

In Bible days, one would put his seal on items for several important reasons. The seal of the Holy Spirit proves:

1. Authenticity of our Salvation
2. Ownership of our Salvation
3. Authority of our Salvation
4. Security of our Salvation
5. Assurance of our Salvation

The Holy Spirit seals us at the moment of salvation.

7. The Holy Spirit Reserves Us.

Ephesians 1:14

"Which is the earnest of our inheritance until the redemption of the purchased possession, unto the praise of his glory."

When you buy a house, you must place a down payment, or earnest money, to reserve the home until the transaction is complete. The Holy Spirit is the earnest of our inheritance. He is the down payment of our salvation until we get to Heaven.

Have you ever made a reservation at a restaurant? The reservation reserves your seats no matter how busy they become or how many people show up.

The Holy Spirit is our proof that our place in Heaven has been reserved.

Philippians 3:20

"For our conversation is in heaven; from whence also we

look for the Saviour, the Lord Jesus Christ:"

The word "conversation" in this verse means citizenship. We are citizens of Heaven!

At the moment of salvation the Holy Spirit reserves us for Heaven.

8. The Holy Spirit Liberates Us.

2 Corinthians 3:17

"Now the Lord is that Spirit: and where the Spirit of the Lord is, there is liberty."

Since the Holy Spirit produces liberty, we are liberated when He moves into our lives. He liberates us from Hell. He liberates us from uncleanness of a sinful heart. He sets us free from the sins that controlled us.

The Spirit breaks the chains of sin that held us captive.

We have been set free with glorious liberty!

Romans 8:21

"Because the creature itself also shall be delivered from the bondage of corruption into the glorious liberty of the children of God."

We have been liberated from the penalty of sin which is eternal death in Hell. We are being liberated from the power of sin through sanctification. We will be liberated from this sinful world when we are glorified.

We must stand fast in the liberty of Christ. Why would we continue to practice the sins from which Christ set us free?

Galatians 5:1

"Stand fast therefore in the liberty wherewith Christ hath made us free, and be not entangled again with the yoke of bondage."

Christian liberty is not a license to sin, but freedom to serve.

Galatians 5:13

"For, brethren, ye have been called unto liberty; only use not liberty for an occasion to the flesh, but by love serve one another.

We must use our liberty in salvation to serve God.

1 Peter 2:16

"As free, and not using your liberty for a cloke of maliciousness, but as the servants of God."

The Holy Spirit liberates us at the moment of salvation.

Salvation is an incredible miracle. All three persons of the Godhead are involved in our salvation. The Father so loved the world that He gave His Son. The Son proved His love for us by dying on the Cross for our sins and raising from the dead. The Holy Spirit works within us to accomplish the wonderful benefits of salvation.

During salvation, the Holy Spirit:

1. Births us.
2. Quickens us.
3. Adopts us.
4. Baptizes us.
5. Indwells us .
6. Seals us.
7. Reserves us.
8. Liberates us.

Have you been born again? If not, all these benefits await your decision.

If you have been saved, thank God for all the incredible things He accomplished in you through the Holy Spirit at the moment you trusted Christ.

10

Activity Of The Holy Spirit AFTER Salvation

The Holy Spirit was active before salvation to bring us to Christ. Also, He participated in the act of our salvation. In this lesson, let's investigate God's Word to learn how the Holy Spirit operates in our lives today as God's children.

1. The Holy Spirit Comforts Us.

John 14:26

> "**But the Comforter, which is the Holy Ghost**, whom the Father will send in my name, he shall teach you all things, and bring all things to your remembrance, whatsoever I have said unto you."

The word translated "Comforter" is the Greek word "paraklētŏs." It could have been translated as an intercessor, consoler, advocate, or helper. I love the wisdom of the Lord

Who chose the word "Comforter." This word encompasses all the previous words but also adds elements of concern, closeness, and fellowship.

Truly, the Holy Spirit is more than strength. He is our Strengthener. He is more than help. He is our Helper. He is more than a comfort. He is our Comforter.

2. The Holy Spirit Teaches Us.

> *John 14:26 "But the Comforter, which is the Holy Ghost, whom the Father will send in my name, **he shall teach you all things**, and bring all things to your remembrance, whatsoever I have said unto you."*

Christ taught His disciples the lofty truths of God. Oh, how I wish we could sit at the feet of Christ and hear His voice as He teaches us. Thankfully, He gave us a teacher His equal.

How can we hope to learn the eternal truths of heaven? How can we finite creatures hope to grasp the infinite? The Holy Spirit is our capable Teacher. He will teach us all things that God needs us to know.

3. The Holy Spirit Reminds Us.

> *John 14:26*
>
> *"But the Comforter, which is the Holy Ghost, whom the Father will send in my name, he shall teach you all things, and **bring all things to your remembrance**, whatsoever I have said unto you."*

We cannot imagine the amount of information known by our infinite and omniscient God. The knowledge contained in the Bible alone is intimidating. The Bible contains what God wants us to know pertaining to life and godliness. Its promises and warnings are true and powerful. Yet, how can we remember all that we need to know?

In His wisdom, God did not leave the job of remembering His transformative teachings to our fickle brains. The Holy Ghost within us will remind us of the truths we need to know when we need to know them. It sets our minds at ease to know that He will give us God's wisdom and remind us of the truths we have studied when needed.

4. The Holy Spirit Guides Us.

John 16:13

*"Howbeit when he, the Spirit of truth, is come, **he will guide you into all truth**: for he shall not speak of himself; but whatsoever he shall hear, that shall he speak: and he will shew you things to come."*

Guide means "to show the way." The Holy Spirit, the Spirit of Truth, will guide us into all truth. He not only teaches us what we need to know, but He also guides us to the truth we need at the right time.

Out of all the things in the Bible, how do we know which one to study? Out of all the things we could learn today, how do we know what we need? The Holy Spirit is our Guide.

5. The Holy Spirit Reveals Us.

John 16:13

*"Howbeit when he, the Spirit of truth, is come, he will guide you into all truth: for he shall not speak of himself; but whatsoever he shall hear, that shall he speak: **and he will shew you things to come.**"*

"He will show you things to come." The Holy Spirit not only reveals the meaning of the written Word of God, but also reveals God's personal will. There is not a book called PAUL

CHAPMAN in the Bible that tells me every decision I should make according to the will of God. Rather, God uses the Holy Spirit to reveal His will to me as I walk in obedience. Furthermore, the Holy Spirit gives discernment, revealing what is going on in the world beyond what we see.

6. The Holy Spirit Inspires Us.

Mark 13:11

"But when they shall lead you, and deliver you up, take no thought beforehand what ye shall speak, neither do ye premeditate: but whatsoever shall be given you in that hour, that speak ye: for it is not ye that speak, but the Holy Ghost."

We are commanded not to worry about what to say when challenged about Christ. Whether it be by wicked men, corrupt judges, or unscrupulous officials, the Holy Spirit will inspire us in the moment. He will give us the words to say when we need them. No doubt, we should be full of Scripture and the Holy Ghost. However, the burden of saying just the right thing does not lie with us, but with the Spirit.

This powerful truth applies in ministry efforts also. The preacher, the teacher, and the soul winner can trust that the Holy Spirit will give them the perfect words to say as they yield to Him.

7. The Holy Spirit Fills us.

Ephesians 5:18

"And be not drunk with wine, wherein is excess; but be filled with the Spirit;"

There's nothing impressive about a balloon with no air in it. Yet, a bouquet of filled balloons changes the atmosphere of a room. The balloon filled with helium will rise above the floor, defying gravity. Likewise, a believer filled with the Holy Spirit rises above the foolishness of the flesh, empowering us to live like Christ.

8. The Holy Spirit Empowers Us.

Acts 1:8

"But ye shall receive power, after that the Holy Ghost is come upon you: and ye shall be witnesses unto me both in Jerusalem, and in all Judaea, and in Samaria, and unto the uttermost part of the earth."

When we are filled with Holy Spirit, we live in power, bearing the fruit of the Spirit in the likeness of Christ. To be filled with the Holy Ghost is to be filled with spiritual power.

We will learn how to be filled with the Spirit in an upcoming chapter.

9. The Holy Spirit Emboldens Us.

Acts 4:31

"And when they had prayed, the place was shaken where they were assembled together; and they were all filled with the Holy Ghost, and they spake the word of God with boldness."

The Holy Spirit is the engine of all spiritual activity in the life of a believer. He emboldened us to witness and empowers us to make an eternal difference.

10. The Holy Spirit Speaks to Us.

Acts 13:2

"As they ministered to the Lord, and fasted, the Holy Ghost said, Separate me Barnabas and Saul for the

work whereunto I have called them."

The Holy Spirit communicates the will of God to the believer. He also teaches us what we need to know. His still, small voice is not audible to the ear but heard in the heart.

We will learn how to discern the voice of the Spirit in a future chapter.

11. The Holy Spirit Sends Us.

Acts 13:4

"So they, being sent forth by the Holy Ghost, departed unto Seleucia; and from thence they sailed to Cyprus."

The Holy Spirit directs the army of God in the world today. He calls people into ministry and directs them where to serve.

12. The Holy Spirit Leads Us.

Romans 8:14

"For as many as are led by the Spirit of God, they are the sons of God."

Luke 4:1

"And Jesus being full of the Holy Ghost returned from Jordan, and was led by the Spirit into the wilderness,"

The Holy Spirit leads us through this life. As a parent holds the hand of a child guiding him through a crowd, so the Holy Spirit leads us. The leading of the Spirit is one of the proofs that we are a child of God.

13. The Holy Spirit Helps Us.

Romans 8:26

"Likewise the Spirit also helpeth our infirmities: for we know not what we should pray for as we ought: but the Spirit itself maketh intercession for us with groanings

which cannot be uttered."

The Holy Spirit is our helper. He assists us in all areas of life. He strengthens our weaknesses, makes up for our lack, and completes us when we are not whole. When we can't, He can.

14. The Holy Spirit Intercedes for Us.

Romans 8:26–27

"Likewise the Spirit also helpeth our infirmities: for we know not what we should pray for as we ought: but the Spirit itself maketh intercession for us with groanings which cannot be uttered. ^{27} And he that searcheth the hearts knoweth what is the mind of the Spirit, because he maketh intercession for the saints according to the will of God."

The Holy Spirit is our prayer partner. He prays with us. He makes sure our prayers are heard, making intercession on our behalf.

15. The Holy Spirit Cheers Us.

Romans 14:17

"For the kingdom of God is not meat and drink; but righteousness, and peace, and joy in the Holy Ghost."

The Holy Spirit is our Heavenly Encourager. He gives us joy in spite of our circumstances as we are filled with Him. Joy is a fruit of the Spirit.

16. The Holy Spirit Gifts Us.

1 Corinthians 12:11

"But all these worketh that one and the selfsame Spirit, dividing to every man severally as he will."

The Holy Spirit gives us special abilities to use in service to God and supernaturally empowers our talents to use for Christ. Have you identified your spiritual gifts?

17. The Holy Spirit Matures Us.

Galatians 5:22–23

"But the fruit of the Spirit is love, joy, peace, longsuffering, gentleness, goodness, faith, [23] Meekness, temperance: against such there is no law."

The Holy Spirit helps us to grow in grace. He matures us in the knowledge and character of Christ. Do you display the fruit of the Spirit in your daily life?

18. The Holy Spirit Strengthens Us.

Ephesians 3:16

"That he would grant you, according to the riches of his glory, to be strengthened with might by his Spirit in the inner man;"

The Holy Spirit strengthens us from the inside out. He provides the inner strength to endure all things and be victorious in the name of Christ.

19. The Holy Spirit Unifies Us.

Ephesians 4:3

"Endeavouring to keep the unity of the Spirit in the bond of peace."

Believers come from separate cultures, different backgrounds, and various philosophies. Nevertheless, the Holy Spirit is the great Unifier making us all one. He gives us unity in spite of our differences.

20. The Holy Spirit Sanctifies Us.

2 Thessalonians 2:13

"But we are bound to give thanks alway to God for you, brethren beloved of the Lord, because God hath from the beginning chosen you to salvation through sanctification of the Spirit and belief of the truth:"

The Holy Spirit gives us victory over sin, setting us apart for Christ's service. As He sanctifies us, we become more like the Master.

21. The Holy Spirit Corrects Us.

Hebrews 12:9

"Furthermore we have had fathers of our flesh which corrected us, and we gave them reverence: shall we not much rather be in subjection unto the Father of spirits, and live?"

The Holy Spirit convicted us of sin, righteousness, and judgment before we were born again. He does the same after we are saved. If we have sin in our lives, or stop obeying the Lord, He corrects us to get us back on track.

22. The Holy Spirit Moves Us.

2 Peter 1:21

"For the prophecy came not in old time by the will of man: but holy men of God spake as they were moved by the Holy Ghost."

The word "moved" in this verse means to be born or carried along. God supernaturally inspired His Word through the writers of Scripture as the Holy Ghost took over, supervising the process. As a writer picks up a pen to write his thoughts, so the Holy Spirit carried these holy men of old to write exactly what God wanted. Nothing more, nothing less.

Have you ever been in the zone? An instance where you lose

track of time, whatever you're doing seems easy, and brings you much joy. The word "moved" has a similar idea.

When God's children are in the right place, at the right time, doing the right thing, with the right spirit, the Holy Spirit can take over and move us as we minister or serve others. Preachers who are filled with the Spirit speak of a sensation at times where they are watching themselves preach or even learning new things as the Holy Spirit empowers their preaching.

We often pray for God to "move" among His people or to "move" during a church service. Thank God for the moving of the Holy Spirit.

23. The Holy Spirit Renews Us.

Titus 3:5

"Not by works of righteousness which we have done, but according to his mercy he saved us, by the washing of regeneration, and renewing of the Holy Ghost;"

2 Corinthians 4:16

"For which cause we faint not; but though our outward man perish, yet the inward man is renewed day by day."

The Holy Spirit renewed our dead spirit and salvation, giving us life. In like manner, He can renew our spirit as it gets worn down in service. The same Spirit Who gave us new life can breathe life into us again when we feel like we can't go on.

God works in the lives of His children through His Holy Spirit. As we yield to the Holy Spirit, allowing Him to fill us, He is free to accomplish His work in us and through us. If we sin against the Holy Spirit, we lose the benefits of His supernatural activity. Most Christians don't know what they lose when choosing sin over the Spirit.

107

When we are filled with the Spirit, we become like Christ. Let's choose to live a supernatural life through the power of the Holy Spirit.

11

Full Of The Holy Ghost

Luke 4:1–2

"And Jesus being full of the Holy Ghost returned from Jordan, and was led by the Spirit into the wilderness, [2] Being forty days tempted of the devil. And in those days he did eat nothing: and when they were ended, he afterward hungered."

To be like Jesus Christ, we must be full of the Holy Ghost. Let's learn about four peoplefour people full of the Holy Ghost and how their examples can encourage us to do the same.

The Holy Ghost is a cCo-equal mMember of the Godhead along with the Father and the Son. When Jesus Christ ascended into Heaven after His resurrection, He sent the Holy Spirit to indwell and empower believers.

John 14:16

"And I will pray the Father, and he shall give you another

Comforter, that he may abide with you for ever;"

John 16:7

"Nevertheless I tell you the truth; It is expedient for you that I go away: for if I go not away, the Comforter will not come unto you; but if I depart, I will send him unto you."

The Holy Ghost is another name for the Holy Spirit. He is active in the world today. His work includes conviction, conversion, and consecration. He indwells, secures, and empowers the children of God.

The Holy Spirit would "come upon" people in the Old Testament, but He did not dwell "in" them. Since Christ paid for our sins, believers are sealed with the Spirit as He indwells them.

Being full of the Holy Ghost does not mean you get more of Him. You received all the Spirit that you will ever need at the moment of salvation. Being filled with the Spirit means that He has all of you.

The Holy Spirit can fill us when we yield to Him. The more we surrender, the more He takes control.

We are commanded to be filled with the Spirit.

Ephesians 5:18

"And be not drunk with wine, wherein is excess; but be filled with the Spirit;"

God would not give us a commandment that we could not know if we were obeying. Therefore, we can know whether we are full of the Holy Ghost. In fact, we are commanded to know! We can notice when others are full of Him as well. Who do you know that is obviously filled with the Spirit?

In an upcoming chapter, we will learn how to be filled with the Spirit.

In this chapter, we will study people who were filled with the Holy Ghost in the New Testament.

1. Jesus Christ was full of the Holy Ghost.

Luke 4:1

"And Jesus being full of the Holy Ghost returned from Jordan, and was led by the Spirit into the wilderness,"

Jesus Christ was full of the Holy Ghost. Everything He accomplished as a man was completed through the power of the Spirit. He is our ultimate example of a Spirit-filled man.

As the sinless Son of God, Christ was filled with the Holy Ghost without measure.

John 3:34

"For he whom God hath sent speaketh the words of God: for God giveth not the Spirit by measure unto him."

In our text, Christ was full of the Holy Ghost as He was led by the Spirit into a great test. You and I will be tested. If we are full of the Holy Ghost, we can overcome any obstacle and withstand any foe with supernatural help.

We must be full of the Holy Ghost to be like Christ. Our Christlikeness is dependent upon our fullness of the Spirit.

2. Early Church deacons were full of the Holy Ghost.

Acts 6:3

"Wherefore, brethren, look ye out among you seven men of honest report, full of the Holy Ghost and wisdom, whom we may appoint over this business."

The Apostles were so busy preaching and praying that the church's responsibility to care for believers in need was not being met. God's solution was to deputize spiritual men to serve so the preachers could focus on preaching the Word and prayer.

Notice that the people who chose these men could identify the ones who were filled with the Spirit. It is obvious!

How can you tell who is full of the Holy Ghost? Here are a few markers of Spirit-fullness.

A. Spirit- filled men are honest and full of wisdom.

Acts 6:3

"Wherefore, brethren, look ye out among you seven men of honest report, full of the Holy Ghost and wisdom, whom we may appoint over this business."

B. The fruit of the Spirit is evident in the lives of those full of the Holy Spirit.

Galatians 5:22–23

"But the fruit of the Spirit is love, joy, peace, longsuffering, gentleness, goodness, faith, ²³ Meekness, temperance: against such there is no law."

C. They will treat people like Christ.

The following verses describe the Spirit-filled believer.

Ephesians 5:18–6:9

"And be not drunk with wine, wherein is excess; but be filled with the Spirit; ¹⁹ Speaking to yourselves in psalms and hymns and spiritual songs, singing and making melody in your heart to the Lord; ²⁰ Giving thanks always for all things unto God and the Father in the name of our Lord Jesus Christ; ²¹ Submitting yourselves one to another in the fear of God.

²² Wives, submit yourselves unto your own husbands, as

unto the Lord. *²³ For the husband is the head of the wife, even as Christ is the head of the church: and he is the saviour of the body. ²⁴ Therefore as the church is subject unto Christ, so let the wives be to their own husbands in every thing. ²⁵ Husbands, love your wives, even as Christ also loved the church, and gave himself for it; ²⁶ That he might sanctify and cleanse it with the washing of water by the word, ²⁷ That he might present it to himself a glorious church, not having spot, or wrinkle, or any such thing; but that it should be holy and without blemish. ²⁸ So ought men to love their wives as their own bodies. He that loveth his wife loveth himself. ²⁹ For no man ever yet hated his own flesh; but nourisheth and cherisheth it, even as the Lord the church: ³⁰ For we are members of his body, of his flesh, and of his bones. ³¹ For this cause shall a man leave his father and mother, and shall be joined unto his wife, and they two shall be one flesh. ³² This is a great mystery: but I speak concerning Christ and the church. ³³ Nevertheless let every one of you in particular so love his wife even as himself; and the wife see that she reverence her husband.*

⁶:¹ Children, obey your parents in the Lord: for this is right. ² Honour thy father and mother; (which is the first commandment with promise;) ³ That it may be well with thee, and thou mayest live long on the earth. ⁴ And, ye fathers, provoke not your children to wrath: but bring them up in the nurture and admonition of the Lord.

⁵ Servants, be obedient to them that are your masters according to the flesh, with fear and trembling, in singleness of your heart, as unto Christ; ⁶ Not with eyeservice, as menpleasers; but as the servants of

Christ, doing the will of God from the heart; [7] With good will doing service, as to the Lord, and not to men: [8] Knowing that whatsoever good thing any man doeth, the same shall he receive of the Lord, whether he be bond or free. [9] And, ye masters, do the same things unto them, forbearing threatening: knowing that your Master also is in heaven; neither is there respect of persons with him."

D. They will have boldness and power to minister.

Acts 4:31–33

"And when they had prayed, the place was shaken where they were assembled together; and they were all filled with the Holy Ghost, and they spake the word of God with boldness. [32] And the multitude of them that believed were of one heart and of one soul: neither said any of them that ought of the things which he possessed was his own; but they had all things common. [33] And with great power gave the apostles witness of the resurrection of the Lord Jesus: and great grace was upon them all."

3. Stephen was full of the Holy Ghost.

Acts 7:55

"But he, being full of the Holy Ghost, looked up stedfastly into heaven, and saw the glory of God, and Jesus standing on the right hand of God,"

Stephen was the first martyr in the Bible. He preached boldly to an angry crowd. He did not shrink from danger. He died as a faithful man of God.

Notice that Stephen looked to Heaven and saw the Lord. People full of the Holy Ghost can see beyond the mortal world. They look to Heaven and see God moving. They are completely surrendered to God's will and way.

114

4. Barnabas was full of the Holy Ghost.

Acts 11:22–24

"Then tidings of these things came unto the ears of the church which was in Jerusalem: and they sent forth Barnabas, that he should go as far as Antioch. ²³ Who, when he came, and had seen the grace of God, was glad, and exhorted them all, that with purpose of heart they would cleave unto the Lord. ²⁴ For he was a good man, and full of the Holy Ghost and of faith: and much people was added unto the Lord."

The name "Barnabas" means "son of consolation." Barnabas was a stable man who brought stability and comfort to every situation. You would have liked to be around Barnabas. He was easy to get along with. He was an encourager. He was full of the Holy Ghost and faith. He was a soul winner who brought many sinners to faith in Christ.

Spirit-filled people are not selfish or carnal. They serve the Lord humbly and gladly.

If you are born again, you can be filled with the Holy Ghost. In fact, you are commanded to be filled with the Spirit. Are you filled with the Spirit?

Let's follow the example of those who were full of the Holy Ghost.

12

Signs Of Holy Spirit Fullness

Ephesians 5:18–21

"And be not drunk with wine, wherein is excess; but be filled with the Spirit; ¹⁹ Speaking to yourselves in psalms and hymns and spiritual songs, singing and making melody in your heart to the Lord; ²⁰ Giving thanks always for all things unto God and the Father in the name of our Lord Jesus Christ; ²¹ Submitting yourselves one to another in the fear of God."

God commands us to be filled with the Holy Spirit. But how can we tell whether we are filled with Him or not? Continue reading to learn the Bible's answer.

There is some confusion in Christendom about the fullness of the Spirit and the evidence of it. For example, Pentecostals and Charismatics misunderstand the doctrine, misconstruing the sign-gift of speaking in tongues as a modern-day evidence of Spirit fullness. This is incorrect. The Bible teaches the liberating truth about this vital doctrine.

What is Holy Spirit Fullness?

Essentially, being filled with the Spirit is being filled with God.

Believers are indwelt and sealed with the Holy Ghost at the moment they are born again. As we humble themselves before God and yield our will to Him, the Holy Spirit is free to accomplish supernatural work in us and through us.

If we exert our own selfish will or partake in sin, the Holy Spirit is hindered from His work and we lose the benefits of His supernatural power.

Just as God will not overcome a sinner's will to forgive his sin and save him from Hell, the indwelling Holy Spirit will not overcome our will to fill and empower us.

We will discuss how to be filled with the Spirit in the chapter entitled "In Pursuit of Power." In this chapter, we will learn how to tell if we are filled with the Holy Ghost.

How can we tell if we are Spirit-filled?

There must be some mechanism by which we can know whether or not we are filled with the Spirit. God would not give us a command that we could not know if we were obeying!

There are two ways to know if you are filled with the Spirit.

A. The Holy Spirit bears witness with your spirit that you are filled.

We know that we are filled with the Spirit in a similar way that we know we are born again. How do we know that we are saved? One important way that we have confidence in our salvation is that the Holy Spirit testifies to our spirit that we are the child of God.

Romans 8:16

"The Spirit itself beareth witness with our spirit, that we are the children of God:"

In like manner, the Holy Spirit communicates with our spirit whether or not we are filled with Him. Simply ask, "Lord, am I filled with your Spirit?" If you are in tune with God, the answer will be clear. If the answer doesn't come quickly, keep asking paying special attention to the still, small voice within you.

The next indication that we are filled with the Spirit is more concrete.

B. The signs of Holy Spirit fullness are visible in your life.

When the Holy Spirit fills you, He changes you. The answer to the following questions is the most obvious way to tell if you are filled with the Spirit. Do you act like it? Do you act like you are filled with God? Are you living more like Jesus?

Only you can answer the question regarding the first way to tell if you are filled with the Spirit. The people around you can help you answer the second question. They will know.

What does a Spirit-filled person look like? How does he act? Thankfully, the Bible gives us the answer.

In Ephesians 5:18 we are commanded to be filled with the Spirit. In the verses following this command, we discover sixteen actions of Spirit-filled believers.

1. Godly Self-Talk.

Each one of us has a voice in our head in which we talk to ourselves. This is called self-talk.

We use self-talk to think about the world, work out problems, and encourage or condemn ourselves. You can tell a lot about yourself or someone else by examining the way they talk to themselves.

The first evidence of Spirit-fullness is talking to yourself about God and His Word.

Ephesians 5:19

"**Speaking to yourselves** in psalms and hymns and spiritual songs, singing and making melody in your heart to the Lord;"

How do you speak to yourself? What do you think about?

One man said, "You will be a success at that which you think about in your spare time." How true!

When we are filled with the Holy Spirit, we cannot help but think about God and His Word.

Colossians 3:16

"Let the word of Christ dwell in you richly in all wisdom; teaching and admonishing one another in psalms and hymns and spiritual songs, singing with grace in your hearts to the Lord."

2. Singing About God.

Ephesians 5:19

"Speaking to yourselves in psalms and hymns and spiritual songs, **singing and making melody in your heart** to the Lord;"

God created us to enjoy and employ music in our daily lives. Music is one of the most powerful elements in our world. It moves our body, soul, and spirit.

God uses sacred music to draw us closer to Him. Satan uses sinful music to draw us away from God. Think about the message and spirit of the music you listen to outside of church. Does it draw you closer to God?

All music is made for worship. What or who does the music you listen to exalt?

A Spirit-filled person sings songs about God. They listen to songs that exalt God.

Our text mentions three types of music.

1. Psalms are the chapters in the middle of the Bible. Psalms is the Israelites inspired songbook.

2. Hymns are songs that honor God and Christ.

3. Spiritual songs are songs about spiritual subjects. They can honor God, uplift Christ, talk about Heaven, encourage believers, etc.

Singing spiritual songs brings us closer to God.

Psalm 100:1–2

"Make a joyful noise unto the LORD, all ye lands. 2 Serve the LORD with gladness: Come before his presence with singing."

Singing sacred songs shows your closeness to God, also. How can you be filled with the Spirit if you don't like spiritual music?

Spiritual music is an integral part of Christianity. Christ sang with His disciples.

Matthew 26:30

"And when they had sung an hymn, they went out into the mount of Olives."

121

3. Singing To The Lord.

Ephesians 5:19 uses two interesting phrases regarding singing.

Notice that the Spirit-filled person sings and makes melody "in their hearts." The person filled with God not only sings out loud, but has a song in their heart!

Music can get stuck in our heart and play on repeat. We have all had an annoying song play over and over in our heads. What a pain! The other side of the coin is that spiritual music that draws you closer to God can play in your heart on repeat. What a blessing!

Observe another important truth in verse nineteen. This singing and melody in our heart is "to the Lord."

Ephesians 5:19

"Speaking to yourselves in psalms and hymns and spiritual songs, singing and making melody in your heart *to the Lord;*"

It is a wonderful thing to sing about God. It is even better to sing TO the Lord.

"Jesus Loves Me" is a song about Christ. "I Love You, Lord Jesus" is a song to Christ.

"He Leadeth Me" is a song about God. "Nearer, My God To Thee" is a song to God.

I enjoy talking to others about my wonderful wife, but it is far better to look into her beautiful green eyes and tell her why I love her.

Learn the joy of singing to God. This is a sign of a Spirit-filled person.

Psalm 105:2

"Sing unto him, sing psalms unto him: Talk ye of all his wondrous works."

4. An Attitude Of Gratitude.

Some Christians are thankful, and some are grumpy complainers. Which one are you? An attitude of gratitude relies on more than personality or circumstance. It is a matter of spirituality.

Spirit-filled Christians are grateful people.

God's children have so much for which to be grateful!

- God gave us life.
- God so loved the world that He made a way of salvation.
- Christ died on the Cross to pay for our sins.
- We have been rescued from eternal damnation and given everlasting life.
- God will never leave us nor forsake us.
- Every morning God gives us new mercies and blessings.

We have been truly blessed!

God's people face difficult trials and temptations in this life. When it rains, the just and the unjust get wet. Certainly, life is not "fair." Everyone has legitimate reason to complain at times. Yet, through it all, the Spirit-filled man focuses more on the blessings than the problems.

A cynical, negative spirit is a red flag that we are not filled with the Spirit. Confess the sin and yield to Him once again.

Whatever we do and in whatever state we are, the Spirit-filled Christian has an attitude of gratitude.

Colossians 3:17

"And whatsoever ye do in word or deed, do all in the name of the Lord Jesus, giving thanks to God and the Father by him."

1 Thessalonians 5:18

"In every thing give thanks: for this is the will of God in Christ Jesus concerning you."

5. A Spirit Of Submission.

Spirit-fullness begins with an emptying of self and a submission to God. It is not surprising that one of the signs of being filled with the Holy Spirit is a spirit of submission.

Spirit-filled people don't fight for their way or desires. Certainly, they will stand for righteousness and fight spiritual battles. However, they do not have a spirit of pride, demanding their own way for their own ends.

Ephesians 5:21

"Submitting yourselves one to another in the fear of God."

The fear of God is the basis of the spirit of submission to one another. God is in control. He will work out the details. He will punish the proud and lift the humble. We must choose to do right.

Proverbs 16:7

"When a man's ways please the LORD, He maketh even his enemies to be at peace with him."

People filled with themselves are full of pride. People satisfied to obey the Lord have the attitude of submission.

Proverbs 14:14

"The backslider in heart shall be filled with his own ways: And a good man shall be satisfied from himself."

Submission is a by-product of humility.

1 Peter 5:5

"Likewise, ye younger, submit yourselves unto the elder. Yea, all of you be subject one to another, and be clothed with humility: for God resisteth the proud, and giveth grace to the humble."

We should submit ourselves to the servants of God and those who are helping us in Jesus' name.

1 Corinthians 16:16

"That ye submit yourselves unto such, and to every one that helpeth with us, and laboureth."

Philippians 2:3

"Let nothing be done through strife or vainglory; but in lowliness of mind let each esteem other better than themselves."

6. Improved Relationships.

When we are full of the Holy Spirit, we will happily fulfill our God-given roles in personal relationships while loving God and treating others as we hope to be treated.

The Bible gives several examples of how we should treat people in different roles. Many of these Bible verses about relationships are given after the command to be filled with the Spirit. Why? Because when we are filled with the Spirit, He empowers us to fulfill our roles and improve our relationships.

Consider the following roles and admonitions in Scripture. Notice that we can live up to these high expectations when we are filled with the Spirit.

Wives

Ephesians 5:22

"Wives, submit yourselves unto your own husbands, as unto the Lord."

Husbands

Ephesians 5:25–29

"Husbands, love your wives, even as Christ also loved the church, and gave himself for it; 26 That he might sanctify and cleanse it with the washing of water by the word, 27 That he might present it to himself a glorious church, not having spot, or wrinkle, or any such thing; but that it should be holy and without blemish. 28 So ought men to love their wives as their own bodies. He that loveth his wife loveth himself. 29 For no man ever yet hated his own flesh; but nourisheth and cherisheth it, even as the Lord the church:"

Children

Ephesians 6:1

"Children, obey your parents in the Lord: for this is right."

Employees

Ephesians 6:5–8

"Servants, be obedient to them that are your masters according to the flesh, with fear and trembling, in singleness of your heart, as unto Christ; 6 Not with eyeservice, as menpleasers; but as the servants of Christ, doing the will of God from the heart; 7 With good will doing service, as to the Lord, and not to men: 8 Knowing

that whatsoever good thing any man doeth, the same shall he receive of the Lord, whether he be bond or free."

Employers

Ephesians 6:9

"And, ye masters, do the same things unto them, forbearing threatening: knowing that your Master also is in heaven; neither is there respect of persons with him."

Church Members

Acts 4:31–33

"And when they had prayed, the place was shaken where they were assembled together; and they were all filled with the Holy Ghost, and they spake the word of God with boldness.

32 And the multitude of them that believed were of one heart and of one soul: neither said any of them that ought of the things which he possessed was his own; but they had all things common. 33 And with great power gave the apostles witness of the resurrection of the Lord Jesus: and great grace was upon them all."

7. Spiritual Power.

Ephesians 6:10

"Finally, my brethren, be strong in the Lord, and in the power of his might."

Spiritual power is a vital sign of being filled with the Spirit.

Notice three types of spiritual power mentioned in conjunction with the Holy Spirit.

A. Power of Protection

The Spirit-filled believer is able to withstand temptation

and spiritual attack.

Ephesians 6:11–16

"Put on the whole armour of God, that ye may be able to stand against the wiles of the devil. [12] For we wrestle not against flesh and blood, but against principalities, against powers, against the rulers of the darkness of this world, against spiritual wickedness in high places. [13]Wherefore take unto you the whole armour of God, that ye may be able to withstand in the evil day, and having done all, to stand. [14] Stand therefore, having your loins girt about with truth, and having on the breastplate of righteousness; [15] And your feet shod with the preparation of the gospel of peace; [16] Above all, taking the shield of faith, wherewith ye shall be able to quench all the fiery darts of the wicked."

B. Power of Confrontation

The believer full of the Holy Spirit uses the Word of God and prayer to conquer devils and win spiritual battles.

Ephesians 6:17–18

"And take the helmet of salvation, and the sword of the Spirit, which is the word of God: [18] Praying always with all prayer and supplication in the Spirit, and watching thereunto with all perseverance and supplication for all saints;"

C. Power of Salvation

The Spirit-filled believer has divine boldness and soul-winning power.

Acts 1:8

"But ye shall receive power, after that the Holy Ghost is come upon you: and ye shall be witnesses unto me both in Jerusalem, and in all Judaea, and in Samaria, and unto the uttermost part of the earth."

The rest of our list of signs of Spirit-fullness is found in Galatians chapter five.

Galatians 5:22–25

"But the fruit of the Spirit is love, joy, peace, longsuffering, gentleness, goodness, faith, ²³ Meekness, temperance: against such there is no law. ²⁴ And they that are Christ's have crucified the flesh with the affections and lusts. ²⁵ If we live in the Spirit, let us also walk in the Spirit."

The fruit of the Spirit is made available to children of God in contrast of the "works" of the flesh. Left to itself, our flesh will produce nothing but the sins listed in Galatians 5:19-21.

Notice that the sins of the flesh are called "works." Work is effort. The result of sinful man's best efforts are sinful works.

Isaiah 64:6

"But we are all as an unclean thing, And all our righteousnesses are as filthy rags; And we all do fade as a leaf; And our iniquities, like the wind, have taken us away."

In contrast, the result of being filled with the Spirit is the "fruit" of the Spirit. These fruits are a product of the Holy Ghost's work in us absent of our effort. Does a fruit tree groan with effort while growing fruit? Does a fruitful vine grumble about how hard it is to bear fruit? Of course not. Fruit grows when the plant is healthy, in the right environment, and with the right nutrients.

Likewise, exercising the fruit of the Spirit is not a result of "trying harder" or "working to be better." The Holy Spirit produces His fruit in us when we get out of His way and yield to His guidance. As sap runs freely through a tree giving it life, so must the Holy Spirit have liberty in our lives as we yield to Him. Only then can we experience His wonderful fruit.

The presence of the fruit of the Spirit is our lives is evidence that we are filled with the Holy Spirit.

Let's learn the rest of the sixteen signs of Spirit fullness.

8. Agape' Love.

There are four types of love found in the Bible. The Greek word agape' (ag-ah´pay) describes God's unconditional and sacrificial love that He has for us and expects us to show to one another.

God's love is more than a feeling. It is a deep commitment to the good and well-being of another at your expense without thought of return.

This supernatural love must flow through us from the Holy Spirit.

Agape' love is a deep commitment and willingness to sacrifice for the benefit of the loved. God loves us and He teaches us to love others with this divine love.

Romans 15:30

"Now I beseech you, brethren, for the Lord Jesus Christ's sake, and for the love of the Spirit, that ye strive together with me in your prayers to God for me;"

Ephesians 5:1–2

"Be ye therefore followers of God, as dear children; ²And walk in love, as Christ also hath loved us, and hath given

himself for us an offering and a sacrifice to God for a sweetsmelling savour."

9. Heavenly Joy.

Joy is gladness from God.

It is different than happiness. Happiness is caused by good things happening to you. Joy is gladness from God regardless of your circumstances.

Happiness is fleeting and uncontrollable. Joy is lasting and available.

If someone gives you $100 that makes you happy. If you lose $100 that makes you sad. Joy allows you to be glad regardless of the balance in your bank account.

Have you ever seen a Christian go through a terrible trial who hasn't lost their sweetness and their smile? That's joy.

God's joy is available. He wants you to have it! It is a by-product of Holy Spirit fullness.

Romans 5:2

"By whom also we have access by faith into this grace wherein we stand, and rejoice in hope of the glory of God."

1 Peter 1:8

"Whom having not seen, ye love; in whom, though now ye see him not, yet believing, ye rejoice with joy unspeakable and full of glory:"

10. Unspeakable Peace.

Peace is the absence of conflict. Peace is the quiet strength and calmness in the midst of chaos.

We have peace with God through the Gospel of Christ.

Romans 5:1

"Therefore being justified by faith, we have peace with God through our Lord Jesus Christ:"

We can have peace in our hearts in the midst of our troubled world.

Philippians 4:7

"And the peace of God, which passeth all understanding, shall keep your hearts and minds through Christ Jesus."

The Holy Spirit calms the distressed heart with quiet and tranquility. Anxiety, fear, and frustration fade as God fills us with feelings of peace, acceptance, and safety.

Our Lord Jesus brought peace to the raging storm on the Sea of Tiberius. He can bring peace to your soul as the Holy Spirit fills you.

11. Superhuman Longsuffering.

Long-suffering is the highest form of patience. It is the supernatural ability to endure injuries, provocations, or problems for a long time. It is the strength to forbear despite difficulty.

Longsuffering people are not easily provoked. They are slow to anger.

Longsuffering people do not quit when they are attacked or when things get difficult.

Colossians 1:11

"Strengthened with all might, according to his glorious power, unto all patience and longsuffering with joyfulness;"

The Holy Spirit strengthens those He fills to supernaturally endure difficulties.

12. Christ-like Gentleness.

Gentleness speaks of kindness. It denotes a sweet disposition and mildness of temper. One who exhibits this evidence of Spirit fullness is not harsh or cruel. They treat others with respect and honor.

2 Corinthians 10:1

"Now I Paul myself beseech you by the meekness and gentleness of Christ, who in presence am base among you, but being absent am bold toward you:"

Christ was gentle as He walked with men. There were times when He preached hard truths or offered severe rebukes, but only when necessary and right.

This fruit of the Spirit fills us with respect and care for others. It drives away grumpiness, irritability, and harshness allowing us to be polite and kind with others.

13. Outward Goodness.

Without Christ, we are all sinners and there is no goodness in us.

Romans 3:10–12

As it is written, There is none righteous, no, not one: 11 There is none that understandeth, there is none that seeketh after God. 12 They are all gone out of the way, they are together become unprofitable; there is none that doeth good, no, not one.

The old man, our flesh, loves to sin. The flesh strives to drive us into sin. But the Holy Ghost can use your life as a vessel to display the glory of God!

The Holy Spirit produces a genuine goodness as we live in this sinful world.

Romans 15:14

"And I myself also am persuaded of you, my brethren, that ye also are full of goodness, filled with all knowledge, able also to admonish one another."

14. Victorious Faith.

Faith is the measure of our personal confidence in God.

Romans 1:17

"For therein is the righteousness of God revealed from faith to faith: as it is written, The just shall live by faith."

At times our faith is weak. Too often our faith fails to move us to obedient action. But thanks be to God for the blessed Holy Ghost Who can fill us with transformational faith in God.

Have you ever wished you had more faith? Allow the Holy Spirit to fill you and you will experience faith like you have never known.

After many days of living on the edge of life and death on a ship in the midst of a terrible storm, most people on the boat had lost hope of escape. They were resigned to death. After a long abstinence in private prayer, the Apostle Paul boldly proclaimed his faith in God.

Acts 27:25

"Wherefore, sirs, be of good cheer: for I believe God, that it shall be even as it was told me."

We can have the same life-changing faith as we are filled with God.

15. Appropriate Meekness.

Meekness is power under control. Christ is the ultimate example of meekness. The Creator lived among His sinful creation. The Saviour could have called legions of angels to set Him free from death. Nevertheless, He became obedient unto the death of the Cross.

We must deal with one another with meekness.

Ephesians 4:2

"With all lowliness and meekness, with longsuffering, forbearing one another in love;"

We must show meekness to all men. Just because you could destroy someone doesn't mean that you should.

Meekness uses the least amount of power necessary to produce the expected result. You don't need to kill a fly with a nuclear bomb. Use a flyswatter. That's meekness.

Titus 3:2

"To speak evil of no man, to be no brawlers, but gentle, shewing all meekness unto all men."

A good Christian is willing to take the short end of the stick in order to please the Lord.

16. Divine Temperance.

Temperance means "self-restraint." We should work to be temperate in all things.

1 Corinthians 9:25

"And every man that striveth for the mastery is temperate in all things. Now they do it to obtain a corruptible crown; but we an incorruptible."

Yet, this spiritual fruit of temperance is not an act of will but a product of Spirit fullness.

Human temperance is limited by human will. Sometimes you don't have enough strength or will power to do what you know to do. When the Holy Spirit gives temperance, it becomes "Spirit-empowered restraint." The Holy Spirit will empower you to do or refrain from doing.

Temperance has always been a theme of Christian preaching. When men realize that they cannot control the flesh in their own strength, it forces them to accept their need for Christ's salvation and His sanctifying work.

We are commanded to be filled with the Holy Spirit, but how can we know if we are filled with Him? The Holy Spirit will bear witness with our spirit and we will display the sixteen signs of Spirit fullness.

1. Godly Self-talk.
2. Singing About God.
3. Singing To The Lord.
4. An Attitude Of Gratitude.
5. A Spirit of Submission.
6. Improved Relationships.
7. Spiritual Power.
8. Agape' Love.
9. Heavenly Joy.
10. Unspeakable Peace.
11. Superhuman Longsuffering.
12. Christ-like Gentleness.
13. Outward Goodness.

14. Victorious Faith.

15. Appropriate Meekness.

16. Divine Temperance.

The Holy Spirit is working in our lives to make us more like Jesus. Christlikeness is the goal of the fullness of the Holy Spirit.

Confess every known sin. Forsake every evil way. Yield to God anew this moment. Reckon yourself dead to sin and alive in Christ. Beg the Holy Spirit to fill you afresh right now.

13

3 Ways To Yield To The Spirit

I pray that it has become clear through this book that we must yield to the Holy Spirit in order to be filled with His power. But what does it look like when we yield to the Spirit?

In this short chapter, let's briefly overview three ways to yield to the Spirit.

1. Pray for Him.

Luke 11:13

"If ye then, being evil, know how to give good gifts unto your children: how much more shall your heavenly Father give the Holy Spirit to them that ask him?"

Prayer is submission. The act of prayer displays our submission to God and our need for His help. When we pray for the power of the Holy Spirit, we humble ourselves. The more we declare our need of Him, the more tender our heart becomes to His direction and the more sensitive we become to His voice.

2. Obey Him.

Acts 5:32

"And we are his witnesses of these things; and so is also the Holy Ghost, whom God hath given to them that obey him."

The Holy Spirit empowers those who obey Him. Obedience and power go hand in hand. The more we obey the Spirit, the more God can trust us with His unlimited power.

3. Submit To Him.

Proverbs 1:23

"Turn you at my reproof: Behold, I will pour out my spirit unto you, I will make known my words unto you."

The more sensitive we become to the Holy Spirit, the more obvious His direction becomes. How do we respond when the Spirit tells us to do inconvenient or uncomfortable things? We must obey the Spirit when He leads us. If we don't submit, we will lose the benefits of His power.

Prayer for power, obedience to God's Word, and surrender to the Spirit's leading are the hallmarks of a Spirit-filled Christian.

14

7 Sins Against The Holy Spirit

Ephesians 4:28–32

"Let him that stole steal no more: but rather let him labour, working with his hands the thing which is good, that he may have to give to him that needeth. Let no corrupt communication proceed out of your mouth, but that which is good to the use of edifying, that it may minister grace unto the hearers. And grieve not the holy Spirit of God, whereby ye are sealed unto the day of redemption. Let all bitterness, and wrath, and anger, and clamour, and evil speaking, be put away from you, with all malice: And be ye kind one to another, tenderhearted, forgiving one another, even as God for Christ's sake hath forgiven you."

The Holy Spirit works through our spirit empowering us to live like Christ and make a difference in the world. If our spirit is not right, the Holy Spirit cannot manifest in us and work through us as God intended.

You must learn the likes and dislikes of the people with whom you plan to have a profitable long-term relationship. A child learns what makes his parents happy or angry. A spouse learns how to make his wife feel loved or unloved. Likewise, we must learn what makes God happy or sad if we plan to have a wonderful relationship with Him. Thankfully, our Lord never changes. His faithfulness ensures we can know what pleases Him or grieves Him any given day.

The Holy Spirit is our connection to God in this age. He lives within us to empower us to live like Christ overcoming the sinful impulses of the flesh. However, Ephesians 4:30 reveals that we can grieve the Holy Spirit, limiting His power within us.

Yes, our spiritual condition and personal actions can limit the Holy Spirit's operation in our lives. The Bible details seven sins that we can commit against the Holy Spirit. Study them thoroughly and strive daily to refrain from sinning.against our divine Helper.

1. Sinners Can BLASPHEME The Holy Spirit.

Matthew 12:31

"Wherefore I say unto you, All manner of sin and blasphemy shall be forgiven unto men: but the blasphemy against the Holy Ghost shall not be forgiven unto men."

Mark 3:29

"But he that shall blaspheme against the Holy Ghost hath never forgiveness, but is in danger of eternal damnation:"

These verses describe the unpardonable sin.

Christians cannot commit the unpardonable sin because

142

they're already pardoned. Only lost sinners who have not been born again can commit the unpardonable sin and blaspheme the Holy Ghost.

What does it mean to blaspheme?

Webster's 1828 Dictionary offers the following definition.

1. To speak of the Supreme Being in terms of impious irreverence; to revile or speak reproachfully of God, or the Holy Spirit. 1 Kings 21. Mark 3.

2. To speak evil of; to utter abuse or calumny against; to speak reproachfully of. Pope.

BLASPHE´ME, *v. i. To utter blasphemy.*

He that shall blaspheme against the Holy Spirit shall not be forgiven. Mark 3.

2. To arrogate the prerogatives of God.

Also, it gives this definition.

BLASPHE´MER, *n. One who blasphemes; one who speaks of God in impious and irreverent terms. 1 Tim. 1.*

Now that we understand what it means to blaspheme, let's apply this knowledge to the blasphemy of the Holy Ghost.

What is the unpardonable sin? It is attributing the work of the Holy Ghost drawing you to saving faith as the work of Satan.

You can blaspheme Jesus Christ and get saved at a later time. Many have done it through the centuries. However, if you continually blaspheme the Holy Ghost, you will never get saved.

It is the Holy Spirit Who brings you to faith in Christ and performs the miracle of the new birth.

Remember the work of the Holy Spirit before salvation from

a previous chapter.

    a. The Holy Spirit Invites Us To Salvation.

    b. The Holy Spirit Draws Us To The Saviour.

    c. The Holy Spirit Convicts us of Sin, Righteousness, and Judgment.

Without these actions, no one can be saved.

If a sinner denies the obvious working of the Holy Spirit, they will reject Christ because they reject the Spirit that is drawing them to Him.

Ultimately, there is one sin that will not be forgiven - rejecting Jesus Christ as your Saviour.

John 3:18

"He that believeth on him is not condemned: but he that believeth not is condemned already, because he hath not believed in the name of the only begotten Son of God."

The true unpardonable sin is the rejection of Christ. Blasphemy of the Holy Ghost provides sinners a reason to reject the Saviour, denying His offer of salvation.

It is the Holy Spirit Who invites us to salvation, draws us to Christ, convicts us of sin, and proves our need to be saved. If one disregards the obvious working of the Holy Spirit, they cannot be saved. Therefore, blaspheming the Holy Ghost is the unpardonable sin.

Perhaps you have seen others in danger of committing the unpardonable sin. Do they see your changed life after salvation and say that you are brainwashed or part of a cult? Do they hear the tug of the Spirit during preaching and claim that the preacher is simply a skilled con man or using manipulation tactics?

Let's warn sinners of the danger of rejecting the Spirit's attempts to save them on the Devil.

2. Anyone Can RESIST the Holy Spirit.

Acts 7:51–53

Ye stiffnecked and uncircumcised in heart and ears, ye do always resist the Holy Ghost: as your fathers did, so do ye. [52] Which of the prophets have not your fathers persecuted? and they have slain them which shewed before of the coming of the Just One; of whom ye have been now the betrayers and murderers: [53] Who have received the law by the disposition of angels, and have not kept it."

These stubborn Jews had a habit of resisting the spiritual workings of the Holy Spirit. In particular, this passage of Scripture warns against resisting the Word of God spoken through His Spirit-empowered ministers. Verse 52 explains that these stubborn Israelites persecuted God's prophets and killed His ministers.

The word "resist" in verse 51 means "to oppose." When we oppose the wisdom, instruction, or correction of Spirit-filled ministers, we resist the Holy Ghost.

In chapter seven, Stephen was a Spirit-filled man preaching the Gospel to the Jews. When they begin to oppose the Gospel, he reminded these stubborn Jews that, like their fathers before them, they were resisting God and His Word.

In the Old Testament, Israelites were called stiff-necked several times by the Lord. They were characterized by their stubborn resistance to the leadership of God.

Exodus 32:9

"And the LORD said unto Moses, I have seen this people, and, behold, it is a stiffnecked people:"

Moses was concerned that the stubborn Israelites would be even more so after his death. He prayed to the Lord asking for forgiveness for their stubbornness.

Exodus 34:9

"And he said, If now I have found grace in thy sight, O Lord, let my Lord, I pray thee, go among us; for it is a stiffnecked people; and pardon our iniquity and our sin, and take us for thine "inheritance.

Deuteronomy 31:27

"For I know thy rebellion, and thy stiff neck: behold, while I am yet alive with you this day, ye have been rebellious against the LORD; and how much more after my death?"

Resisting the Holy Spirit leads to destruction.

Nehemiah 9:30

"Yet many years didst thou forbear them, and testifiedst against them by thy spirit in thy prophets: yet would they not give ear: therefore gavest thou them into the hand of the people of the lands."

Stubbornness and rebellion characterize the human condition to this day.

Stiff-necked unbelievers will not yield to the Gospel of Christ. Some sinners are so obstinate that they would rather kill God's messengers than submit to their Creator. Most sinners would never stoop to murder. However, they are willing to persecute Spirit-filled servants of the Saviour by attacking their character, questioning their motives, or destroying their reputation.

Also, many professing Christians are obstinate, living in

rebellion against God and His Word.

Stiff-necked Christians refused to put their neck in the yoke of service with Christ. As a result, they don't receive help with their burdens or joy in their journey.

Matthew 11:28–30

"Come unto me, all ye that labour and are heavy laden, and I will give you rest. [29] Take my yoke upon you, and learn of me; for I am meek and lowly in heart: and ye shall find rest unto your souls. [30] For my yoke is easy, and my burden is light."

If we resist the Holy Ghost, we lose all the benefits of His blessed activity in our lives.

The Christian life is one of surrender and sacrifice. Holy Spirit fullness begins with yielding our will to God. We must not resist the Holy Spirit's work in our lives if we hope to please the Lord and fulfill His will.

3. We can LIE to the Holy Spirit.

Acts 5:1–4

"But a certain man named Ananias, with Sapphira his wife, sold a possession, [2] And kept back part of the price, his wife also being privy to it, and brought a certain part, and laid it at the apostles' feet. [3] But Peter said, Ananias, why hath Satan filled thine heart to lie to the Holy Ghost, and to keep back part of the price of the land? [4] Whiles it remained, was it not thine own? and after it was sold, was it not in thine own power? why hast thou conceived this thing in thine heart? thou hast not lied unto men, but unto God."

At the end of Acts chapter four, Barnabas sold a piece

of property and left it at the Apostles' feet for the care of suffering Christians. This made him a local hero. Ananias and Sapphira had a piece of property that they decided to sell and give to the Apostles for the same purpose. Somewhere in this process, Satan gave them the idea to keep some of the money from the sale. Normally, this would not be wrong, but they had committed publicly to give the entire proceeds to the Lord. Instead of rejecting the sinful idea of Satan to keep some money, they chose to act on it, breaking their promise to the Lord. When they brought the money, they acted as if it was the entire proceeds. Like Adam and Eve, this husband and wife had agreed together to sin against the Lord.

Their sin was twofold:

1. They listened to the lies of Satan instead of the righteous guidance of the Holy Spirit.

2. They attempted to deceive the Spirit-filled Apostles.

Our Holy Lord took offense at their attempt of deception. He said they had lied to the Holy Ghost. Their judgment was a swift and severe example to the rest of the congregation.

This account is a powerful reminder that we cannot lie to God. We may deceive friends, family, and acquaintances, but we can never deceive the Lord. He knows all and sees all.

Proverbs 15:3

"The eyes of the LORD are in every place, Beholding the evil and the good."

Hebrews 4:13

"Neither is there any creature that is not manifest in his sight: but all things are naked and opened unto the eyes of him with whom we have to do."

Satan is the father of lies.

John 8:44

"Ye are of your father the devil, and the lusts of your father ye will do. He was a murderer from the beginning, and abode not in the truth, because there is no truth in him. When he speaketh a lie, he speaketh of his own: for he is a liar, and the father of it."

When Satan subtly places the idea in our hearts to lie, we must reject his unholy influence and yield to the divine guidance of the Holy Spirit.

Consider some ways modern Christians can lie to the Holy Ghost.

1. Making a public spiritual commitment then backing out.

2. Lying to Spirit-filled leaders.

3. Making a private spiritual commitment and reneging on the promise.

4. Attempting to hide sin from the Lord.

We must never lie to the Holy Ghost.

4. Believers Can QUENCH the Holy Spirit.

1 Thessalonians 5:19

"Quench not the Spirit."

The word quench means "to extinguish." We are commanded to protect the work of the Holy Spirit in our lives and not quench it.

The Holy Spirit is likened to a flame.

Matthew 3:11

"I indeed baptize you with water unto repentance: but he

that cometh after me is mightier than I, whose shoes I am not worthy to bear: he shall baptize you with the Holy Ghost, and with fire:"

Acts 2:3

"And there appeared unto them cloven tongues like as of fire, and it sat upon each of them."

We quench the Holy Spirit the same way we put out any other fire. Fire needs fuel and oxygen to burn. If you remove either, the fire will go out.

The priests in the Old Testament tabernacle were commanded to keep the fire that God had started burning. They were to never let it go out.

During the ministry of Eli, the lamp of God was in danger of going out. Eli was getting old and unable to accomplish all the work of the ministry. His sons, Hophni and Phineas, were wicked and more concerned about satisfying their fleshly lusts rather than serving the Lord. God raised up young Samuel to protect the fire of the Lord.

We must be like Samuel. We must protect the flame of the Holy Ghost within us. We must stoke the fire and add the fuel to make sure it keeps burning brightly.

The fuel of the Holy Spirit is the Word of God. The Holy Spirit empowers the Word of God in our lives. The more we are filled with God's Word, the more we can be filled with God's Spirit. If you don't add the Word of God to your life, your spiritual fire will go out.

The oxygen of the Holy Spirit is prayer. We are commanded to pray in the Holy Ghost. As we pray in surrender to God, it gives oxygen for the Holy Spirit to burn brightly in our lives. If we do not pray, our spiritual fire will be quenched.

The fastest way to put out a fire is to pour water on it. We must be careful not to pour water on the work of the Holy Spirit in our lives.

The context of 1 Thessalonians 5:19 contains commandments concerning the Christian life. They give us insight on how we can quench the Holy Spirit.

Consider the following ways we can quench the Holy Spirit in our lives from 1 Thessolonians chapter five.

1. Disrespect those we are to esteem. Verse 13

2. Fight amongst ourselves. Verse 13

3. Join in with the unruly. Verse 14

4. Discourage the faint-hearted. Verse 14

5. Render evil for evil. Verse 15

6. Choose to complain. Verse 16

7. Failed to pray. Verse 17

8. Protest your circumstances withoutgratitude. Verse 18

9. Snub the preaching of God's Word. Verse 20

10. Do what you want in self-will rather than proving what is right and wrong by the will of God and doing it. Verse 21

11. Take no thought for our Christian testimony. Verse 22

The Holy Spirit is constantly working in our lives. Anytime we reject His leadership through sin, stubbornness, or self-will, we quench the fire, stopping His supernatural work.

Surrender your will daily and walk in the Spirit. Only then will you enjoy Christian victory over the things of this world and experience the supernatural power of living in the Spirit.

5. Christians Can GRIEVE the Holy Spirit.

Ephesians 4:30

"And grieve not the holy Spirit of God, whereby ye are sealed unto the day of redemption."

This verse is one of the most convicting verses in the Bible regarding the Holy Spirit. It proves that it is possible for us to grieve the Holy Spirit. The word grieve means "to afflict with sorrow: to make sad or sorrowful." This verb does not occur anywhere else in the New Testament.

It is a sobering thought to think that we can cause pain and grief to the Holy Spirit of God within us!

How can we grieve the Holy Spirit? By sin.

Sin not only quenches the supernatural working of the Holy Spirit, but also it grieves Him in His heart. He so desperately wants to empower us to live like Christ and experience all the blessings that God has to offer that He is grieved when we choose sin over God.

The context of Ephesians 4:30 gives a list of the sins that grieve the Holy Spirit. Of course, any sin unconfessed will grieve the Holy Spirit. Nevertheless, the sins listed are the most common offenders.

Let's list some sins from Ephesians chapter four that grieve the Holy Spirit so we can cleanse our lives from them and protect our divine Helper.

1. Lying. Verse 25

2. Unrighteous anger. Verse 26

3. Laziness and theft. Verse 28

4. Corrupt communications. Verse 29

5. Bitterness. Verse 31

6. Wrath and anger. Verse 31

7. Clamor and evil speaking. Verse 31

8. Malice or evil intentions. Verse 31

9. Unforgiveness. Verse 32

Any sin of the hands or the heart will grieve the Holy Spirit. When we grieve the Holy Spirit, we tie His hands as He shrinks into our spirit in paralyzed sadness. The Holy Spirit can only return in power when we confess and forsake our sin.

Search your heart today. Ask God to reveal any wicked way in you. Confess every known sin. Apologize to the Holy Spirit for offending Him. Ask Him to fill you afresh with His power and help you be like Jesus. Only then will we know the supernatural power of living in the Holy Spirit.

6. Christians Can TEMPT The Holy Spirit.

Acts 5:9

"Then Peter said unto her, How is it that ye have agreed together to tempt the Spirit of the Lord? behold, the feet of them which have buried thy husband are at the door, and shall carry thee out."

The word "tempt" in Acts 5:9 means "to prove or test."

Ananias and Sapphira dared to put the Holy Ghost on trial, whether He's able to discern the thoughts of the hearts or punish evil doers. They learned the hard way that He can.

The Israelites tempted God.

Psalm 78:40

"How oft did they provoke him in the wilderness, And grieve him in the desert!"

Psalm 78:56

"Yet they tempted and provoked the most high God, And kept not his testimonies:"

Psalm 95:9–11

"When your fathers tempted me, Proved me, and saw my work. [10] Forty years long was I grieved with this generation, And said, It is a people that do err in their heart, And they have not known my ways: [11] Unto whom I sware in my wrath That they should not enter into my rest."

Consider this passage from Exodus that teaches us a few ways the Israelites tempted the Lord.

Exodus 17:2–7

"Wherefore the people did chide with Moses, and said, Give us water that we may drink. And Moses said unto them, Why chide ye with me? wherefore do ye tempt the LORD? [3] And the people thirsted there for water; and the people murmured against Moses, and said, Wherefore is this that thou hast brought us up out of Egypt, to kill us and our children and our cattle with thirst?

[4] And Moses cried unto the LORD, saying, What shall I do unto this people? they be almost ready to stone me. [5] And the LORD said unto Moses, Go on before the people, and take with thee of the elders of Israel; and thy rod, wherewith thou smotest the river, take in thine hand, and go.

[6] Behold, I will stand before thee there upon the rock in Horeb; and thou shalt smite the rock, and there shall come water out of it, that the people may drink. And Moses did so in the sight of the elders of Israel.

[7] And he called the name of the place Massah, and Meribah, because of the chiding of the children of Israel,

and because they tempted the LORD, saying, Is the LORD among us, or not?"

There are three important lessons we learn from this passage of Scripture.

A. The Israelites tempted the Lord by doubting His provision.

Exodus 17:2

"Wherefore the people did chide with Moses, and said, Give us water that we may drink. And Moses said unto them, Why chide ye with me? wherefore do ye tempt the LORD?"

Days after their miraculous deliverance from bondage in Egypt, the Israelites came to a place where there was not enough water for the people and animals. Immediately they begin to fight with Moses and complain against God. They were upset that God was not providing for their needs as they saw them. Had they looked through the eyes of faith, they would have seen that God brought them to a dry place so He could miraculously provide their needs and show them He was still going to take care of them.

Don't tempt God by complaining and doubting when you don't have enough. Trust Him to provide what you need. He may not give you everything you want, but He will provide what you need in His time. If He did not provide it, then you must not need it yet.

B. The Israelites tempted the Lord by doubting His purpose.

Exodus 17:3

"And the people thirsted there for water; and the people

murmured against Moses, and said, Wherefore is this that thou hast brought us up out of Egypt, to kill us and our children and our cattle with thirst?"

These doubting Jews got so worked up that they begin to wonder if God brought them to this place to kill them. How foolish! How could they forget the great purpose God had for them? He delivered them from Egypt because He had mighty works for them to accomplish. They were His chosen people, after all.

Never forget that God has a great purpose for you. You are in existence because He wanted you to be. As long as you're breathing, God is not done with you yet. When things get tough, don't tempt God by doubting His love or His plan.

C. The Israelites tempted the Lord by doubting His presence.

Exodus 17:7

"And he called the name of the place Massah, and Meribah, because of the chiding of the children of Israel, and because they tempted the LORD, saying, Is the LORD among us, or not?"

How could they question the Lord's presence? He had just protected them through the ten plagues of Egypt. He had delivered them with a high hand out of bondage. They had walked through the parted sea and watched the mighty army of Egypt drown.

How soon we forget the blessings of God! Don't question God's presence when things get tough. He has promised to never leave you nor forsake you. Trust His word and lean on His faithfulness.

New Testament believers are warned not to tempt Christ.

1 Corinthians 10:9

"Neither let us tempt Christ, as some of them also tempted, and were destroyed of serpents."

Don't put God on trial. Stop demanding that He prove Himself over and over.

It's a foolish thing to tempt God. He will do exactly what He promised in His Word. He will punish sin exactly as He warned. He will reward the righteous precisely as He promised. He is exactly who He says He is.

Likewise, it is a sin to tempt the Holy Spirit. Never doubt His power. Stop wondering if He will be with you. Don't test His holiness by partaking in sin.

Simply yield to Him and trust Him. He will do exactly what He promised to do.

7. The Holy Spirit Can Be VEXED.

Isaiah 63:10

"But they rebelled, and vexed his holy Spirit: Therefore, he was turned to be their enemy, and he fought against them."

The Hebrew word for "vexed" in this verse is often translated "grieved" in the Old Testament. However, the meaning in this context is deeper than simple grief. Vexed is a stronger word than grieved. Consider the following *Webster's 1828 Dictionary* definition for vexed.

1. To irritate; to make angry by little provocations; a popular use of the word.

2. To plague; to torment; to harass; to afflict.

3. To disturb; to disquiet; to agitate.

To grieve the Holy Spirit is to cause pain and sorrow. To vex the Holy Spirit is to go beyond grief to anger. In our text, we see that the Israelites continued in rebellion after so many blessings that they vexed the Holy Spirit until He turned against them. It is a terrible thing when the God who desires to bless you must fight against you because of sin and stubbornness.

God cannot allow His children to continue in sin without consequences. When we continue in sin despite God's mercy and grace, He must chastise us for our good and for His glory.

Hebrews 12:5–11

"And ye have forgotten the exhortation which speaketh unto you as unto children, My son, despise not thou the chastening of the Lord, nor faint when thou art rebuked of him: [6] *For whom the Lord loveth he chasteneth, and scourgeth every son whom he receiveth.* [7] *If ye endure chastening, God dealeth with you as with sons; for what son is he whom the father chasteneth not?* [8] *But if ye be without chastisement, whereof all are partakers, then are ye bastards, and not sons.* [9] *Furthermore we have had fathers of our flesh which corrected us, and we gave them reverence: shall we not much rather be in subjection unto the Father of spirits, and live?* [10] *For they verily for a few days chastened us after their own pleasure; but he for our profit, that we might be partakers of his holiness.* [11] *Now no chastening for the present seemeth to be joyous, but grievous: nevertheless afterward it yieldeth the peaceable fruit of righteousness unto them which are exercised thereby."*

As a good Father, God must chastise His disobedient children. If a professed believer can continue in unrepentant sin without correction, he is not a child of God.

The Holy Spirit seals believers until the day of redemption. That fact means that He is a captive of our poor decisions. He cannot escape our self-willed decisions and sinful choices.

We grieve the Holy Ghost when we sin. If we continue in unrepentant sin, His sorrow turns to anger. Each sin is an irritation. Every iniquity is a provocation to wrath.

Once He is vexed, the Holy Spirit will stop working through you and will start working on you to bring you to a place of submission. Just as He is a captive to our sin, we are a captive to His correction. There is no where you can run to hide from the Holy Spirit who lives within you. He was made to be your comforter and helper. You don't want to find out what it's like for Him to fight against you with all the power of divinity.

Matthew 21:44

"And whosoever shall fall on this stone shall be broken: but on whomsoever it shall fall, it will grind him to powder."

When we come to God in surrender and brokenness, He will strengthen us and bind us together. When we fight against God in self-will and rebellion, He will chastise us and grind us to powder until we surrender.

The Holy Spirit within us longs to empower us supernaturally. But he is a gentleman. He will only help us when we ask. He will only fill us when we are ready.

The Holy Spirit is sensitive. When we sin against the Holy Spirit, we lose the benefits of all His supernatural work. Commit today to live a clean and holy life before the Lord so you can know the supernatural benefits of living in the power of the Holy Spirit.

15

In Pursuit Of Power

Luke 24:49

"And, behold, I send the promise of my Father upon you: but tarry ye in the city of Jerusalem, until ye be endued with power from on high."

Ephesians 5:18

"And be not drunk with wine, wherein is excess; but be filled with the Spirit;"

God has not left you helpless as you travel through this life. There is a power available for you that transcends all that you see and know. It is greater than any earthly circumstance or human frailty. This power works in the believer, transforming him into a little Christ. How can one so like his sinful earthly father be conformed into the likeness of his sinless Heavenly Father? This power! How could rugged and unlearned fishermen such as Peter, James, and John become great Apostles that would change the world? This power! The same power is available to you today.

This Power Comes from the Fullness of the Holy Spirit.

Jesus did not leave us comfortless when He ascended to Heaven. Truthfully, He said it was better for Him to go so we could have the Comforter. Believe God's Word! It is better for the Holy Spirit of God to dwell in you than if Jesus was on Earth today and you were walking by His side! And yet, the Holy Ghost is ignored, quenched, and grieved by most of God's people. They live as if there was no Holy Spirit at all. How sad!

In this chapter, we will investigate the Scripture to find out how to obtain the fullness of the Holy Spirit and this transformative spiritual power.

Did you think of the Holy Spirit today? Did you yield to Him? Are you in tune to His promptings? Are you filled with His power?

Confess your sin. Humble yourself. Declare your need of Him. Ask to be filled with the sweet Holy Spirit as you pour out yourself to God in prayer.

I do not offer myself as a model of one who has attained the fullness of God's power. Although I have had glorious glimpses of it, I am woefully deficient. I fail far too often. I am too filled with self. I am too unwilling to sacrifice. I am too stubborn at times.

Certainly, I am not a guru or master of the subject, but I have been on a journey in pursuit of God's power since I was 17 years old.

I heard the sermons of old that moved cities. I read the biographies of Spirit-filled men that shook nations.

In D.L. Moody's testimony, his ministry multiplied after

He was filled with the Holy Ghost. He preached the same sermons that used to bring dozens to Christ, but after He was filled with this spiritual power, the same sermons brought hundreds to saving faith.

Jack Hyles told the story of begging to be filled with the Spirit's power lying on his dead father's grave who went to Hell after listening to his son's powerless sermons. At Bro. Hyles' funeral, I prayed all night in the auditorium begging for spiritual power.

In the last thirty years, I have fasted hundreds of days and prayed countless hours in search of this power. I have studied God's Word relentlessly on the subject.

God, in His great mercy, has allowed me to experience the fullness of the Spirit and spiritual power at times. Once you know what it's like to be filled with the Spirit, you will never be the same. You will sense the emptiness when you are full of self. You will never be satisfied with mediocrity again.

We could talk for days of spirit-filled men who made a difference in the world. Do you have a hunger for God's power? Do you thirst to be filled with the Spirit?

What is spiritual power?

Two main Greek words are translated "power" in the New Testament.

The first word for power is "exousi'a." It means authority.

Authority is a type of power. Consider the following illustration.

An 80,000 pound cement truck is driving down the highway at 65 mph. It has raw power. A full-grown man would never have enough physical strength to stop it. Now, picture a 185-pound state trooper step into the highway in front of the cement truck, motioning for it to pull over. The truck begins to slow down immediately and pulls to a stop at the side of the road in front of the trooper. Why? The truck had more power, but the state trooper had more authority.

God has given us authority! We must live and minister in the authority of Christ.

The second Greek word for power is "dunamis." It means force or miraculous power. It is the root word where we get the word dynamite. It means explosive power.

Back to our previous illustration. A state trooper has authority over a truck, but no authority over a boulder. If a state trooper commands a boulder to move, it will stay because the trooper doesn't have enough power to move it. However, if you put a stick of dynamite under the boulder, the raw power will do the work. God has given us both authority and explosive power. We must learn to walk in both authority and power to fulfill God's plan.

Follow this progression of Bible principles as we lay a foundation in pursuit of God's power.

Power belongs to God.

Matthew 6:13

"And lead us not into temptation, but deliver us from evil: For thine is the kingdom, and the power, and the glory, for ever. Amen."

Christ has all power. He is willing to share it with His followers.

Matthew 28:18–20

"And Jesus came and spake unto them, saying, All power is given unto me in heaven and in earth. ¹⁹ Go ye therefore, and teach all nations, baptizing them in

the name of the Father, and of the Son, and of the Holy Ghost: [20] Teaching them to observe all things whatsoever I have commanded you: and, lo, I am with you alway, even unto the end of the world. Amen."

Christ gave power to His disciples.

Luke 9:1

"Then he called his twelve disciples together, and gave them power and authority over all devils, and to cure diseases."

Luke 10:19

"Behold, I give unto you power to tread on serpents and scorpions, and over all the power of the enemy: and nothing shall by any means hurt you."

The apostles served Christ with "great power."

Acts 4:33

"And with great power gave the apostles witness of the resurrection of the Lord Jesus: and great grace was upon them all."

Stephen was full of power.

Acts 6:8

"And Stephen, full of faith and power, did great wonders and miracles among the people."

Paul accomplished miracles "by the power of the Spirit of God."

Romans 15:19

"Through mighty signs and wonders, by the power of the Spirit of God; so that from Jerusalem, and round about unto Illyricum, I have fully preached the gospel of Christ."

Spiritual power cannot be bought with money.

There are no short cuts to spiritual power. It must be earned by following the Biblical formula.

Acts 8:18–19

"And when Simon saw that through laying on of the apostles' hands the Holy Ghost was given, he offered them money, [19] Saying, Give me also this power, that on whomsoever I lay hands, he may receive the Holy Ghost."

Christ warned the disciples not to attempt His spiritual work in the power of the flesh. They were commanded to make the pursuit of power a priority by waiting for it to come.

Luke 24:49

"And, behold, I send the promise of my Father upon you: but tarry ye in the city of Jerusalem, until ye be endued with power from on high."

God fills believers with His power; the same power that raised Jesus Christ from the dead.

Ephesians 1:19–20

"And what is the exceeding greatness of his power to us-ward who believe, according to the working of his mighty power, [20] Which he wrought in Christ, when he raised him from the dead, and set him at his own right hand in the heavenly places,"

We are called by the power of God.

Ephesians 3:7

"Whereof I was made a minister, according to the gift of the grace of God given unto me by the effectual working of his power."

We are strengthened by God's glorious power to accomplish His work.

Colossians 1:10–11

That ye might walk worthy of the Lord unto all pleasing, being fruitful in every good work, and increasing in the knowledge of God; [11] Strengthened with all might, according to his glorious power, unto all patience and longsuffering with joyfulness;"

2 Thessalonians 1:11

"Wherefore also we pray always for you, that our God would count you worthy of this calling, and fulfil all the good pleasure of his goodness, and the work of faith with power:"

2 Timothy 1:7

"For God hath not given us the spirit of fear; but of power, and of love, and of a sound mind."

Some professors of faith in Christ have a form of godliness, but deny its true power. Don't follow their example.

2 Timothy 3:5

"Having a form of godliness, but denying the power thereof: from such turn away."

Where does this power originate?

The Holy Ghost is the source of our spiritual power. To be filled with the Holy Ghost is to be filled with power.

Acts 1:8

"But ye shall receive power, after that the Holy Ghost is come upon you: and ye shall be witnesses unto me both in Jerusalem, and in all Judaea, and in Samaria, and unto

the uttermost part of the earth."

Acts 10:38

"How God anointed Jesus of Nazareth with the Holy Ghost and with power: who went about doing good, and healing all that were oppressed of the devil; for God was with him."

Micah 3:8

"But truly I am full of power by the spirit of the LORD, And of judgment, and of might, To declare unto Jacob his transgression, And to Israel his sin."

Romans 15:13

"Now the God of hope fill you with all joy and peace in believing, that ye may abound in hope, through the power of the Holy Ghost."

Romans 15:19

"Through mighty signs and wonders, by the power of the Spirit of God; so that from Jerusalem, and round about unto Illyricum, I have fully preached the gospel of Christ."

1 Corinthians 2:4

"And my speech and my preaching was not with enticing words of man's wisdom, but in demonstration of the Spirit and of power:"

How do we receive this supernatural power?

I have listened to many sermons on the power of God. I have read many books and biographies about God's power. Yet, good men who display the power of the Spirit have disagreed about how to get it. Is it something you must earn? It is something you simply claim?

I went to the Bible to find the answers. There is a formula for God's power. There is a map in the Scriptures for those seeking His power to follow.

1. Seeking

Isaiah 44:3

"For I will pour water upon him that is thirsty,And floods upon the dry ground: I will pour my spirit upon thy seed, And my blessing upon thine offspring:"

The first step to being filled with Holy Spirit power is to seek it. You must know that it is available and decide that you want it. God does not give His power easily or cheaply. You must thirst for it and begin a lifetime journey to increase it in your life.

I have not arrived, but I have been seeking the fullness of the Spirit and supernatural power for almost 30 years.

Are you thirsty for God's Spirit? Do you long to know His presence and power? Are you going to pay the price for His supernatural strength? Then, let the journey begin!

2. Surrender

Ephesians 5:18

"And be not drunk with wine, wherein is excess; but be filled with the Spirit;"

Spiritual power begins with a sincere seeking of the fullness of the Spirit. The next step to be filled with the Spirit is surrender. Andrew Murray said, "Being filled with the Spirit is simply this - having my whole nature yielded to His power. When the whole soul is yielded to the Holy Spirit, God Himself will fill it."

You cannot fill a glass with water if it is already full of motor oil. Likewise, we cannot be filled with the Holy Spirit if we are already full of sin and self-will.

We must yield ourselves completely to God. Confess every sin. Declare every iniquity. Seek and destroy anything between you and your God. Surrender your life. Give Him your heart. Promise Him your future. Tell Him there's nothing that you would not do for Him. Only then can you be filled with the Spirit and power.

3. Supplication

Luke 11:13

"If ye then, being evil, know how to give good gifts unto your children: how much more shall your heavenly Father give the Holy Spirit to them that ask him?"

In this graduate level sermon on prayer, our Lord taught us that the Father will give the Holy Spirit to them that ask Him. Why should we pray for the Holy Ghost? Doesn't He indwell us at the moment of salvation? Of course. This petition is not for the Spirit to indwell us, rather it is a supplication for Him to fill us and empower us.

We must pray for the Holy Spirit to fill us. As we humble ourselves, we must beg Him to empower us to be like Christ. We must pray the price.

Pray daily for the Holy Spirit to fill you. Beg Him repeatedly to manifest His power through you. Don't settle for a fleshly life. Cry out in desperation to be made anew in the image of Christ as you live each day.

4. Scripture

Luke 4:32

"And they were astonished at his doctrine: for his word

was with power."

The word of God is powerful. It can save souls and change lives.

We will have more spiritual power as we use more Scripture in our lives. Speak it. Live it. Teach it. Build your life upon it. God's eternal Word is without equal.

The Gospel is "the power of God unto salvation."

Romans 1:16

"For I am not ashamed of the gospel of Christ: for it is the power of God unto salvation to every one that believeth; to the Jew first, and also to the Greek."

The Word of God and the Spirit of God are linked. To have more of one is to have more of the other. The Holy Spirit inspired and empowered the Word of God.

Acts 10:44

"While Peter yet spake these words, the Holy Ghost fell on all them which heard the word."

Ephesians 6:17

"And take the helmet of salvation, and the sword of the Spirit, which is the word of God:"

We must be filled with Scripture to be filled with the Spirit.

5. Sanctification

The Holy Spirit can only fill and empower a holy vessel. Sin grieves the Holy Spirit. If we hope to have His power, we must remove any known sin from our lives.

2 Timothy 2:19–21

"Nevertheless the foundation of God standeth sure, having this seal, The Lord knoweth them that are his.

And, Let every one that nameth the name of Christ depart from iniquity. [20] But in a great house there are not only vessels of gold and of silver, but also of wood and of earth; and some to honour, and some to dishonour. [21] If a man therefore purge himself from these, he shall be a vessel unto honour, sanctified, and meet for the master's use, and prepared unto every good work."

Choose to live a separated life. Reject the sinful whims and ways of this present world. Realize that laying aside sin allows you to pick up God's power.

2 Corinthians 7:1

"Having therefore these promises, dearly beloved, let us cleanse ourselves from all filthiness of the flesh and spirit, perfecting holiness in the fear of God."

Surrender immediately when the Holy Spirit points out a sin in your life. When we respond to His correction, He pours out more of His power. If we reject His correction in stubbornness, we lose His benefits.

Proverbs 1:23

"Turn you at my reproof: Behold, I will pour out my spirit unto you, I will make known my words unto you."

We must reject any sin that would quench or grieve the Holy Spirit if we hope to live in His power.

6. Starvation

Matthew 17:21

"Howbeit this kind goeth not out but by prayer and fasting."

Fasting is an important step in the pursuit of power. Starving yourself from the normal pleasures of life sets you apart from this world, allowing you to tune in to the spiritual world. Refraining from food or sleep quickly reminds you of the weakness of the flesh. Allow each hunger pain of a fast to be a prayer for God's power and fullness.

Denial of fleshly pleasure loosens the hold of the sin nature on you. It allows you to see things through a spiritual lens. There is no substitute for prayer and fasting and the pursuit of power and fullness of the Holy Ghost.

When is the last time you skipped a meal in search of spiritual power?

7. Suffering

We must be willing to suffer as we seek God's power.

Christ went into temptation full of the Holy Ghost. He was led by the Spirit into the wilderness to be tempted of the Devil.

Luke 4:1

"And Jesus being full of the Holy Ghost returned from Jordan, and was led by the Spirit into the wilderness,"

After our Lord endured the temptation successfully, He returned in the power of the Spirit.

Luke 4:14

"And Jesus returned in the power of the Spirit into Galilee: and there went out a fame of him through all the region round about."

During Christ's temptation, Satan promised Him a shortcut to power.

Luke 4:6

"And the devil said unto him, All this power will I give thee, and the glory of them: for that is delivered unto me;

and to whomsoever I will I give it."

However, the only way to receive God's power is to obediently endure suffering and temptation. There are no shortcuts to Holy Spirit fullness.

2 Corinthians 12:9

"And he said unto me, My grace is sufficient for thee: for my strength is made perfect in weakness. Most gladly therefore will I rather glory in my infirmities, that the power of Christ may rest upon me."

Can you truly know Christ and His power until you have suffered with Him?

Philippians 3:10

"That I may know him, and the power of his resurrection, and the fellowship of his sufferings, being made conformable unto his death;"

2 Timothy 1:8

"Be not thou therefore ashamed of the testimony of our Lord, nor of me his prisoner: but be thou partaker of the afflictions of the gospel according to the power of God;"

God knows His people are weak. He knows that we are flesh and remembers that we are but dust. He will only give His life-changing power to those He can trust. Every time we endure suffering or overcome temptation, we earn the right for more power by proving our faithfulness.

Study the Spirit-filled men of the past. Each of them had a cross to bear. The deeper the suffering, the greater the power. Are you willing to suffer to be used of God mightily?

8. Service

What is a parent's first question when a child asks for money? "What are you going to do with it?"

Why should God give you His power? What will you do with it?

A desire to honor God by fulfilling your role as father, mother, parent, child, spouse, sibling, church member, or minister, is a good reason to request Holy Spirit power.

Spiritual service gives God a reason to bless you with increased power. Consider the following acts of service that give God a reason to grant your request.

A. Preaching

1 Corinthians 1:18

"For the preaching of the cross is to them that perish foolishness; but unto us which are saved it is the power of God."

1 Corinthians 2:4–5

"And my speech and my preaching was not with enticing words of man's wisdom, but in demonstration of the Spirit and of power: 5 That your faith should not stand in the wisdom of men, but in the power of God."

B. Winning souls

Acts 1:8

"But ye shall receive power, after that the Holy Ghost is come upon you: and ye shall be witnesses unto me both in Jerusalem, and in all Judaea, and in Samaria, and unto the uttermost part of the earth."

Matthew 28:18–20

"And Jesus came and spake unto them, saying, All power is given unto me in heaven and in earth. 19 Go ye therefore, and teach all nations, baptizing them in the name of the Father, and of the Son, and of the Holy Ghost: 20 Teaching them to observe all things whatsoever I have commanded you: and, lo, I am with you alway, even unto the end of the world. Amen."

C. Striving to be like Christ

1 Corinthians 1:24

"But unto them which are called, both Jews and Greeks, Christ the power of God, and the wisdom of God."

There is no greater goal than to be like Christ! The ultimate goal of the Christian life is to be like Jesus.

God will not grant you His eternal power without good reason. Earnestly beg the Holy Spirit to fill you so you can honor God by serving Him. Each time you get out of your comfort zone in the name of Christ, He will grant you more power.

God will only provide a miracle when you attempt things for God that need one. When is the last time you got out of your comfort zone in the name of Jesus? When is the last time you attempted something that required special strength or power from God? He will grant power to you as you need it. Serve Christ in such a way that you need His supernatural power every day.

Let's get practical. Apply the truths in this chapter in the following ways as you seek God's power.

1. Confess your desire to be filled with the Spirit.

2. Surrender your will to God fully and completely.

3. Pray for the filling of the Holy Spirit every morning and throughout the day.

4. Read, study, memorize, and quote God's Word.

5. Ask the Holy Spirit if there is any sin in your life that you need to confess and forsake.

6. Plan a fast to seek for God's power.

7. Run to God when trials and temptation attempt to seduce you to sin.

8. Give God good reasons to fill you with His power as you seek to win souls, be like Jesus, and serve Him in the church.

I have not attained the fullness of power, but I am seeking it. I have not arrived, but, like you, I am on a journey.

Are you seeking God's supernatural power?

Do you sense your need of something more?

Do you want to see more people saved?

Do you want God to move mightily while you serve Him?

Practice the eight disciplines above and learn what it means to be filled with the Holy Ghost and with power.

There is unlimited power available to you. Start walking the path today to the Spirit-filled life today.

16

Discerning The Voice Of The Holy Spirit

1 Samuel 3:1–10

"And the child Samuel ministered unto the LORD before Eli. And the word of the LORD was precious in those days; there was no open vision. ²And it came to pass at that time, when Eli was laid down in his place, and his eyes began to wax dim, that he could not see; ³And ere the lamp of God went out in the temple of the LORD, where the ark of God was, and Samuel was laid down to sleep; ⁴That the LORD called Samuel: and he answered, Here am I. ⁵And he ran unto Eli, and said, Here am I; for thou calledst me. And he said, I called not; lie down again. And he went and lay down. ⁶And the LORD called yet again, Samuel. And Samuel arose and went to Eli, and said, Here am I; for thou didst call me. And he answered, I called not, my son; lie down again. ⁷Now Samuel did not yet know the LORD, neither was the word of the LORD

yet revealed unto him. ⁸ And the LORD called Samuel again the third time. And he arose and went to Eli, and said, Here am I; for thou didst call me. And Eli perceived that the LORD had called the child. ⁹ Therefore Eli said unto Samuel, Go, lie down: and it shall be, if he call thee, that thou shalt say, Speak, LORD; for thy servant heareth. So Samuel went and lay down in his place. ¹⁰ And the LORD came, and stood, and called as at other times, Samuel, Samuel. Then Samuel answered, Speak; for thy servant heareth."

We must learn how to discern the voice of the Holy Spirit so we can live the supernatural life.

In this amazing passage, little Samuel is approached by God Himself. God speaks to Samuel, but Samuel does not recognize His voice. Samuel had never heard God before. He didn't know what God sounded like.

Samuel thought Eli had called him. When Samuel asked Eli what he wanted, Eli told Samuel that he had not called him and to go lie back down. Eventually, Eli realized that God was talking to Samuel. Eli knew the voice of God. Thankfully, he was there to teach Samuel how to recognize it and what to do about it.

There are many Christians who do not know how to discern the voice of God. Let's look at the Scriptures and learn this important truth.

The Bible offers instances in which the Holy Spirit speaks.

The Holy Ghost speaks to teach.

Ezekiel 11:5

"And the Spirit of the LORD fell upon me, and said unto me, Speak; Thus saith the LORD; Thus have ye said, O

house of Israel: for I know the things that come into your mind, every one of them."

The Holy Spirit speaks to lead.

Acts 8:29

"Then the Spirit said unto Philip, Go near, and join thyself to this chariot."

The Holy Spirit speaks to reveal.

Acts 10:19

"While Peter thought on the vision, the Spirit said unto him, Behold, three men seek thee."

The Holy Spirit speaks to invite.

Revelation 2:7

"He that hath an ear, let him hear what the Spirit saith unto the churches; To him that overcometh will I give to eat of the tree of life, which is in the midst of the paradise of God."

The Holy Spirit speaks to separate for service.

Isaiah 48:16

"Come ye near unto me, hear ye this; I have not spoken in secret from the beginning; From the time that it was, there am I: And now the Lord GOD, and his Spirit, hath sent me."

Acts 13:2

"As they ministered to the Lord, and fasted, the Holy Ghost said, Separate me Barnabas and Saul for the work whereunto I have called them."

Acts 20:28

"Take heed therefore unto yourselves, and to all the flock, over the which the Holy Ghost hath made you overseers, to feed the church of God, which he hath purchased with his own blood."

The Holy Spirit speaks to forbid.

Acts 16:6–7

"Now when they had gone throughout Phrygia and the region of Galatia, and were forbidden of the Holy Ghost to preach the word in Asia, ⁷ After they were come to Mysia, they assayed to go into Bithynia: but the Spirit suffered them not."

Examine the following passages that show the Holy Spirit speaking.

God spoke to Elijah. Elijah knew the voice of God.

1 Kings 19:9–13

"And he came thither unto a cave, and lodged there; and, behold, the word of the LORD came to him, and he said unto him, What doest thou here, Elijah? ¹⁰ And he said, I have been very jealous for the LORD God of hosts: for the children of Israel have forsaken thy covenant, thrown down thine altars, and slain thy prophets with the sword; and I, even I only, am left; and they seek my life, to take it away. ¹¹ And he said, Go forth, and stand upon the mount before the LORD. And, behold, the LORD passed by, and a great and strong wind rent the mountains, and brake in pieces the rocks before the LORD; but the LORD was not in the wind: and after the wind an earthquake; but the LORD was not in the earthquake: ¹² And after the earthquake a fire; but the LORD was not in the fire: and after the fire a still small voice. ¹³ And it was so, when

Elijah heard it, that he wrapped his face in his mantle, and went out, and stood in the entering in of the cave. And, behold, there came a voice unto him, and said, What doest thou here, Elijah?"

Notice that the voice of God speaking to a person's heart is not loud like a windstorm. It does not shake the earth like an earthquake. It is not bright and hot like a fire.

The voice of God is a still, small voice. The word "still" means quiet. The word "small" means thin or soft.

Compare the account of God speaking on Mount Sinai.

Exodus 20:18–22

"And all the people saw the thunderings, and the lightnings, and the noise of the trumpet, and the mountain smoking: and when the people saw it, they removed, and stood afar off. ¹⁹ And they said unto Moses, Speak thou with us, and we will hear: but let not God speak with us, lest we die. ²⁰ And Moses said unto the people, Fear not: for God is come to prove you, and that his fear may be before your faces, that ye sin not. ²¹ And the people stood afar off, and Moses drew near unto the thick darkness where God was. ²² And the LORD said unto Moses, Thus thou shalt say unto the children of Israel, Ye have seen that I have talked with you from heaven."

When God spoke on Mount Sinai, it was loud, terrifying, and accompanied by fire. When God speaks to the heart, it is a still, small voice.

The Holy Spirit of God will lift His voice in your heart rarely. He will not demand you listen. He will speak in a quiet voice. Therefore, you must be sensitive to it lest you miss it.

God spoke to the congregation in a loud, booming voice. He

speaks to the individual in a still, small voice.

Here are a few tips to discern the voice of the Holy Spirit in your heart.

1. Ask God to speak to you every day.

2. Expect God to communicate you through His Spirit.

3. A calm heart and quiet mind help us to hear the Spirit.

4. Learn to tell the difference between self-talk and the Spirit. The voice of the Spirit is similar to the voice of self-talk within us, but it is identifiable as the Spirit.

5. The voice of the Holy Spirit always agrees with Scripture.

6. The voice of the Spirit will encourage you to do what the Bible says is right.

7. The voice of the Spirit will instruct you to live like Jesus.

How can we have a better relationship with Holy Spirit?

Practice these steps every day.

1. Be aware of the Spirit.

2. Sense His presence.

3. Listen for His still, small voice.

4. Yield to Him often.

5. Submit to His correction.

6. Pray for filling.

7. Take every opportunity to serve the Lord trusting the Holy Spirit to empower you.

Are you ready to take the next step. Try this Spiritual exercise:

Psalm 46:10

"Be still, and know that I am God: I will be exalted among the heathen, I will be exalted in the earth."

You can learn to discern the Holy Spirit's voice from a place of stillness. Still the mind. Calm the heart.

The exercise will go over some of your heads. It will feel weird at first to most of you. It is not a New Age gimmick. Try it several times and see if it makes a difference in your sensitivity to the Holy Spirit.

1. Close your eyes.

2. Take a deep breath. Feel the air go deep into your lungs as your diaphragm expands.

3. Pay attention to your breath. As you exhale, feel the stress and tension drain from your shoulders.

4. As you breathe deeply two more times, feel the tension release from the rest of your body.

5. Continue to breathe purposefully, focusing on your breath.

6. Move your attention to your mind. Picture all the thoughts of your mind crying for attention as lazy clouds passing in a calm blue sky. Each cloud represents a thought, a worry, a task. You can choose to grab on to any thought, but you just let them all pass by. Watch them move along. Your mind is still and quiet.

7. Now move your thoughts to your body. Feel your arms, your legs, your hands, and feet. Squeeze all your muscles tightly together for three seconds and release and relax

them as if someone flipped a switch. Notice the tension leave your body. Your body is more relaxed than it has been in quite a while. Thank God for your body as it is the temporary home of your eternal soul.

8. Move your thoughts deeper inward to the soul. Your thoughts, will, and emotion live here. Thank God that you can think and feel and know and desire. Now give all of these things to Him. Surrender your very being to Christ. Ask Him to fill you with the mind of Christ. Tell Him you want to think like He thinks and feel like He feels.

9. Move deeper inward to your spirit. This is your connection to God. You feel close to God here - free from the layers of noise in the world around you. Sense your connection to God. He is in you. He is not 1,000,000 miles away in Heaven. He is right here. You can hear him. You can know Him.

10. Now look one step deeper. In your spirit resides the Holy Spirit. You can sense His presence within you. You can hear His voice. He is Christ in you, the hope of glory. He is the fullness of God within you. He is all power in all wisdom there to assist you through this life.

11. Now yield. Ask Him to fill you as you surrender yourself completely.

12. Tune in to that still, small voice. Turn the spiritual dial of your spirit to that frequency where the Holy Ghost broadcasts. Yield to His voice. Surrender your thoughts and your will. Ask Him to speak to you. Ask Him specific questions. Tell Him what you need. And when you leave this place of stillness, leave your spirit tuned to His voice.

Just as there are countless radio waves passing around us right now, the Holy Spirit is speaking. We cannot hear those radio and TV broadcasts because we are not to tuned into them.

Likewise, many Christians cannot hear the Holy Spirit because they are not tuned into His voice. Use the tools from this chapter to discern that still, small voice that will lead you, guide you, and empower you supernaturally through this life.

17

God's Supernatural Book

Psalm 119:89–104

"LAMED. For ever, O LORD, Thy word is settled in heaven. [90] Thy faithfulness is unto all generations: Thou hast established the earth, and it abideth. [91] They continue this day according to thine ordinances: For all are thy servants. [92] Unless thy law had been my delights, I should then have perished in mine affliction. [93] I will never forget thy precepts: For with them thou hast quickened me. [94] I am thine, save me; For I have sought thy precepts. [95] The wicked have waited for me to destroy me: But I will consider thy testimonies. [96] I have seen an end of all perfection: But thy commandment is exceeding broad. [97] MEM. O how love I thy law! It is my meditation all the day. [98] Thou through thy commandments hast made me wiser than mine enemies: For they are ever with me. [99] I have more understanding than all my teachers: For *thy testimonies are my meditation.* [100] *I understand more than the ancients, Because I keep thy precepts.* [101] *I have refrained my feet from every evil way, That I might keep thy word.* [102] *I have not departed from thy judgments: For thou hast taught me.* [103] *How sweet are thy words unto my taste! Yea, sweeter than honey to my mouth!* [104]*Through thy precepts I get understanding: Therefore I hate every false way."*

The Holy Bible is a book of miracles and it is a miracle book. There is no doubt that the Bible is different than other books. Let's discover some amazing facts about God's supernatural Book!

Psalm 119 explains the many ways that God's Word is special. Verse 89 reveals that God's Word is supernatural. It is "for ever settled in Heaven." God wrote the Bible in eternity past and gave it to mankind in sections by forty different authors over more than 1,000 years.

In this passage of Scripture, we learn that the Bible is:

- eternal. vs 89
- faithful. vs 90
- delightful and protective. vs 92
- unforgettable. vs 93
- life-giving. vs 93
- worth seeking. vs 94
- worth considering. vs 94
- speaks about many subjects. vs 96
- worthy of our love. vs 97
- profitable for meditation. vs 97
- able to make wise the simple. vs 98
- always with us. vs 98
- able to give understanding at any age. vs 99

- worthy of obedience. vs 100
- our guide for right and wrong. vs 101,104
- sweet and satisfying to the soul. vs 103

Truly, the Bible is a supernatural book!

President Ronald Reagan pointed to the miraculous Bible and said, "Indeed, it is an indisputable fact that all the complex and horrendous questions confronting us at home and worldwide have their answer in that SINGLE BOOK."

Abraham Lincoln said, "I believe the Bible is the best gift God has ever given to man. All the good from the Saviour of the world is communicated to us through this Book."

Napoleon said about God's supernatural Word, "... is no mere book, but A LIVING CREATURE that conquers all that face it".

The word Bible simply means "book." But this is no ordinary book. It is the "Holy Bible." It is the sacred Book of the Creator. It's the only book that God ever wrote.

The Bible has appealed to people from every tribe and nation throughout the ages. No other book has so changed individuals and transformed societies. Yet, this book has a unity and cohesion that leaves a discerning person only one logical explanation: There is one author and that author is God Almighty.

In this chapter, we will look at five ways the Bible is miraculous.

1. The Bible's Supernatural REALITY.

The Bible is different than every other book. Consider the following facts about God's miraculous Book:

The Reality of The Bible's Preeminence

- The Bible claims to be written by God Almighty.

191

• Almost 2.5 billion people in the world claim the Bible as Holy Book of God. That is over 1/3 of the people on the planet.

• The first book ever printed on a moveable type press was the Bible.

• More Bibles have been printed than any book in the history of the world.

• The Bible is the best-selling book every year. It is excluded from bestselling book lists because it would always rank the highest.

• Over 100 million Bibles are printed every year.

• Robert Aitken's Bible (The King James Version without the Apocrypha) was the first English Bible printed in America.

• Over 90% of Americans own at least one Bible, whether as a gift or a purchase, but only 12% read it daily.

• It is estimated that the average American owns 9 Bibles.

• Bible sales earn more than $400 million every year.

• Over 60,000 people use a Bible app on their phones at any given moment.

• Three people every second share some form of Biblical quote or verse to their social media outlets.

• According to the Guiness Book of World Records over 5 billion copies of the Bible have been sold since 1851. To put this in perspective, the next best-selling book of all time is 'Don Quixote' by Miguel de Cervantes which has sold over 500 million copies.

- Guinness estimates that in the last 2,000 years over 5 trillion copies of the Bible have been printed.

- You can read the Bible out loud in less than 80 hours at a leisurely, but consistent pace.

- The Bible has inspired more song lyrics than any other book.

- On a humorous note, the Bible is the most shoplifted book in the world. I guess the thieves have never read as far as the Ten Commandments!

- The influence of the King James Bible on our culture cannot be overestimated. Many common phrases originated in the Bible such as "When I was a child, I spake as a child"; "Eat, drink, and be merry"; "From strength to strength"; "By the skin of our teeth"; "salt of the earth"; "Our Father, which art in heaven"; "A house divided against itself cannot stand"; "A drop in the bucket"; "A scapegoat"; "A behemoth" -and many more.

- The full Bible has been translated into 532 languages. It has been partially translated into 2,883 languages.

The Reality of The Bible's Perfection

Consider the following facts about how perfectly the Bible is constructed.

- 2 testaments
- 66 books
- 39 books in the Old Testament
- 27 books in the New Testament
- 1,189 chapters
- 31,102 verses

- 788,258 words (not including the Hebrew alphabet in Psalm 119 or the superscriptions listed in some of the Psalms)

- 3,116,480 letters

- Psalms is the longest book by chapters. Jeremiah is the longest book by words.

- 3 John is the shortest book by verses. 2 John is the shortest book by words.

- The longest chapter is Psalm 119 with 176 verses.

- The shortest chapter is Psalm 117 with two verses.

- The longest verse in the Bible is Esther 8:9.

- The shortest verse in the Bible is John 11:35.

- "Mahershalalhashbaz" is the longest word in the Bible. It is found in Isaiah 8:3.

- There are at least 185 songs in the Bible. 150 songs are in the book of Psalms.

- The Bible was written:

- over a 1500-year span (from circa 1400 B.C to A.D. 100)

- Over 40 generations

- Over 40 authors from many walks of life

- In different places

- At different times

- On three continents (Asia, Africa, and Europe)

- In three languages (Hebrew, Aramaic [Chaldee], and Greek)

- The middle verses of the Bible are Psalm 103:1-2.

Bless the LORD, O my soul: and all that is within me, bless his holy name. Bless the LORD, O my soul, and forget not all his benefits:

- The first phrase of the Bible is "In the beginning God..."

- The last word of the Bible is "Amen."

- Dataset mapping has identified 63,779 cross-references built into God's Word, making the Bible the world's first hyper-linked book.

2. The Bible's Supernatural HISTORY.

The Holy Bible is the history book of the Universe. God revealed Himself to mankind in the Garden of Eden. For thousands of years, the Creator spoke to mankind through dreams, visions, angels, or Old Testament appearances of Christ. Unfortunately, God's people would only hear new information from God at random intervals.

In His infinite wisdom, God chose to give us a written record of historical events and principles for life.

2 Peter 1:3–4

"According as his divine power hath given unto us all things that pertain unto life and godliness, through the knowledge of him that hath called us to glory and virtue: 4 Whereby are given unto us exceeding great and precious promises: that by these ye might be partakers of the divine nature, having escaped the corruption that is in the world through lust."

The written Word of God is more reliable than dreams and visions.

2 Peter 1:14–21

"Knowing that shortly I must put off this my tabernacle,

even as our Lord Jesus Christ hath shewed me. [15] *Moreover I will endeavour that ye may be able after my decease to have these things always in remembrance.* [16] *For we have not followed cunningly devised fables, when we made known unto you the power and coming of our Lord Jesus Christ, but were eyewitnesses of his majesty.* [17] *For he received from God the Father honour and glory, when there came such a voice to him from the excellent glory, This is my beloved Son, in whom I am well pleased.* [18] *And this voice which came from heaven we heard, when we were with him in the holy mount.* [19] *We have also a more sure word of prophecy; whereunto ye do well that ye take heed, as unto a light that shineth in a dark place, until the day dawn, and the day star arise in your hearts:* [20] *Knowing this first, that no prophecy of the scripture is of any private interpretation.* [21] *For the prophecy came not in old time by the will of man: but holy men of God spake as they were moved by the Holy Ghost."*

The LORD instructed Moses to write His Word.

Exodus 17:14

"And the LORD said unto Moses, Write this for a memorial in a book, and rehearse it in the ears of Joshua: for I will utterly put out the remembrance of Amalek from under heaven."

Exodus 34:27

"And the LORD said unto Moses, Write thou these words: for after the tenor of these words I have made a covenant with thee and with Israel."

Like Isaiah and Jeremiah, God chose men throughout history and inspired them to write the eternal words of God.

Isaiah 30:8

"Now go, write it before them in a table, And note it in a book, That it may be for the time to come For ever and ever:"

Jeremiah 36:2

"Take thee a roll of a book, and write therein all the words that I have spoken unto thee against Israel, and against Judah, and against all the nations, from the day I spake unto thee, from the days of Josiah, even unto this day."

Consider these facts about the historicity of the Word of God.

- The Bible was written over a 1500-year span (from circa 1400 B.C to A.D. 100)

- It was written over 40 generations.

- God used 40 authors from many walks of life.

- Portions of Scripture were written in different places and on three continents (Asia, Africa, and Europe).

- Portions of Scripture were written in three languages (Hebrew, Aramaic [Chaldee], and Greek).

- Portions of the Bible are over 3,500 years old.

- God inspired the Bible and promised to preserve it from corruption of man.

Psalm 12:6–7

"The words of the LORD are pure words: As silver tried in a furnace of earth, purified seven times. ⁷ Thou shalt keep them, O LORD, Thou shalt preserve them from this generation for ever."

God ordained that His inspired and preserved Word would be published broadly and spread to every generation.

Psalm 68:11

"The Lord gave the word: Great was the company of those that published it."

History is full of incredible examples of the history of God's Word. For example, there is a Bible in the University of Gottingen that is written on 2,470 palm leaves.

The Bible is the most verified and studied book in the history of mankind. It's provenance and history are without reasonable question.

3. The Bible's Supernatural ACCURACY.

The Bible was written over a period of 1500 years, in over 40 generations, by over 40 authors from many walks of life on three continents (Asia, Africa, and Europe), in three languages (Hebrew, Aramaic [Chaldee], and Greek) and it agrees completely with itself. The Bible is the perfect Book of God without errors.

Of course, copies of the Bible have been printed with errors. For example, a Bible was printed in 1631 that left out the word "not." What difference can one word make? The text said, "Thou shalt commit adultery." What?? It is famously called The Wicked Bible or The Sinner's Bible. Many modern Bible verses contain grievous errors. However, God has ensured that His Word is available without error to every generation.

One man wrote the following. Emphasis mine.

"The Bible, compared with all other ancient writings, has MORE MANUSCRIPT EVIDENCE than any TEN pieces of classical literature COMBINED! Although originally written on perishable materials, having to be re-copied by hand for thousands of years before the invention of the printing press, it's style, correctness and accuracy

has been preserved as no other book in all History! The Jews had special classes of scholars within their culture whose sole duty was to preserve and transmit the books of the Bible with PERFECT accuracy, counting the very consonants, vowels, syllables and words per manuscript as a means of double-checking. Literally THOUSANDS of ancient manuscripts in the original languages have been unearthed which PROVE, beyond a shadow of a doubt, that the Scriptures have come down through the ages to us just as they were originally written!"

Here is another quote.

"Historians who wrote during the times the Bible was written unknowingly confirmed the accuracy of Scripture.

There were several secular historians who wrote about the events of the New Testament at the same time the Bible was being written. Josephus is the most well-known of them. He was a Jewish historian. Tacitus was a Roman historian who would have no benefit from not telling the truth. Both these men, as well as others, can be used to back up the historical accuracy of the Bible.

There are historical discoveries regularly coming to light that continue to support the accuracy of the Bible. Merrill Unger, who compiled a Bible dictionary wrote, **"Old Testament archeology has rediscovered whole nations, resurrected important peoples, and in a most astonishing manner filled in historical gaps, adding immeasurably to the knowledge of Biblical backgrounds."**

https://www.whatchristianswanttoknow.com/10-amazing-bible-facts/#ixzz6mP0jZfJT

The Bible is supernaturally accurate!

Consider the Bible's Supernatural Knowledge.

The Bible was written thousands of years ago. We are so much smarter than the writers of the Bible were, right? With their limited knowledge, what could they possibly have known?

God inspired His men to give us information thousands of years before it was discovered by modern science.

Day & Night At The Same Time

Luke 17:30

"Even thus shall it be IN THE DAY when the son of man is revealed. (vs 31) IN THAT DAY . . . (vs 34) I tell you, IN THAT NIGHT . . . "

Nobody in Luke's day thought it could be day and night at the same time! They thought the earth was flat! Luke was written around 65 A.D. How did Luke know something that the scientists didn't know until the 16th century? The Bible is inspired by God.

The Earth Is Round

Isaiah 40:22

"It is he that sitteth upon the circle of the earth, And the inhabitants thereof are as grasshoppers; That stretcheth out the heavens as a curtain, And spreadeth them out as a tent to dwell in:"

How did Isaiah know in 700 B.C. the Earth is round? The scientists of Isaiah's day thought the earth was flat. They didn't discover the Earth is round until the early 1500s when Magellan sailed around the world. God revealed that the Earth was round 2000 years ahead of science.

The Earth Hangs In Space

Job 26:7

"He stretcheth out the north over the empty place, And hangeth the earth upon nothing."

". . . and hangeth the earth upon nothing." During the time of Job, nobody believed the earth "hangeth upon nothing!" Job is the oldest book in the Bible! Written over 3500 years ago! How did Job know something that was IMPOSSIBLE to know during his day? He was inspired by God.

Genesis 2:7

"And the LORD God formed man of the dust of the ground, and breathed into his nostrils the breath of life; and man became a living soul."

Many people don't take Genesis 2:7 seriously. In November 1982, Reader's Digest had an article titled "How Life on Earth Began." It stated that according to scientists at NASA's Ames Research Center, the ingredients needed to form a human being can be found in clay. The article said,"The Biblical scenario for the creation of life turns out to be not far off the mark."(Reader's Digest, November, 1982 p.116) No, the Bible hit the mark!

The Currents In the Seas

Psalm 8:8

"The fowl of the air, and the fish of the sea, And whatsoever passeth through the paths of the seas."

". . . whatsoever passeth through the PATHS OF THE SEAS." After reading Psalm 8:8, Matthew Maury, a U.S. Naval officer, set out to locate these curious "paths in the seas." He discovered the oceans have paths which flow through them.

He became known as the "pathfinder of the seas". How did David (the writer of Psalms) know, over 2,000 years ago, there were "paths in the seas"? God inspired him to write it.

The Cycle of Condensation and Evaporation

Ecclesiastes 1:7

"All the rivers run into the sea; yet the sea is not full; unto the place from whence the rivers come, thither they return again."

How did the writer of Ecclesiastes know the water cycle of condensation and evaporation? The sun evaporates water from the ocean and the water vapor rises and becomes clouds. This water in the clouds falls back to the Earth as rain, collects in rivers, and makes its way back to the ocean. This wasn't known until Galileo in 1630! How did the writer of Ecclesiastes know this in 1000 B.C. 2500 YEARS AHEAD OF SCIENCE?

Wash in Running Water

Leviticus 15:13

"And when he that hath an issue is cleansed of his issue; then he shall number to himself seven days for his cleansing, and wash his clothes, and bathe his flesh in running water, and shall be clean."

God said to wash the infected flesh in RUNNING WATER. Science didn't discover that until two men named Pasteur and Koch in the late 1800s. Doctors were washing their hands in a bowl of water and spreading the germs like wildfire. It wasn't until the invention of the microscope and the science of bacteriology that doctors started washing under RUNNING WATER. Leviticus was written around 1490 B.C.! SCIENCE WAS ABOUT 3000 YEARS BEHIND!

The Knowledge of Wind Patterns and Jet Streams

Ecclesiastes 1:6

"The wind goeth toward the south, and turneth about unto the north; it whirleth about continually, and the wind returneth again according to his circuits."

How did the writer of Ecclesiastes know the wind traveled within circuits? How did he know something that the aerologists and meteorologists are just now understanding?

Importance Of The Blood

Leviticus 17:11

"For the life of the flesh is in the blood: and I have given it to you upon the altar to make an atonement for your souls: for it is the blood that maketh an atonement for the soul."

That's the most accurate, scientific statement ever written about the blood!

It is the blood that carries on all the life processes of the body. It is the blood that causes growth, builds new cells, grows bone and flesh, stores fat, makes hair and nails. It is the blood that feeds and supports all the organs of the body. If the blood supply be cut off from an arm, that arm will immediately begin to die and rot. It is the blood that repairs the body. It is the blood that clots wounds, that grows new flesh, new skin and even new nerves. It is the blood that fights disease.

For thousands of years, doctors treated people by a practice called "bleeding." They thought illnesses could be cured by removing blood. In 1799, only 200 years ago, George Washington was literally bled to death. They bled poor George four times and the last time they took over a quart of his blood!

They didn't know, but they were literally draining away his life by removing his blood. It wasn't until the early 1900's that a man named Dr. Lister discovered that the blood provides the body's immune system - THE LIFE OF THE FLESH IS IN THE BLOOD!

Don't you find these facts amazing? What Moses wrote in 1490 B.C., the brightest minds man can produce, are just now discovering! How can the Bible, written thousands of years ago, by men with such limited knowledge, be so far ahead of the best mankind can produce in 6,000 years?

How does God's Word compare to other religious texts?

To realize how amazing that Book is compare what the scientists taught when the Word of God was written. They believed lightning bolts were missiles from the gods. The Vedas (Hindu sacred book) taught that to get rain, tie a frog with his mouth open to a tree and repeat some magic words - and presto - rain! The Egyptians believed stars were the souls of dead people who were now gods. The Greeks believed a god named Atlas held the earth on his shoulders. Some taught the Earth sat on the backs of several large (very large!) elephants. And the elephants were resting on the back of a large (very, very large!) turtle! And the turtle? He was resting on a large (very, very, very large!) snake! And the snake? Well, you get the picture.

Our supernatural Bible contains nothing so foolish despite what was taught and believed during the writers' days! The Bible says, "And Moses was learned in all the wisdom of the Egyptians. . ." (Acts 7:22) And yet, the "superstitions and mythology" of Egypt are not in the books written by Moses! In fact, after 6,000 years of "discoveries and advancements" - the supernatural Word of God can stand beside the most advanced medical, scientific, and historical books available!

4. The Bible's Supernatural PROPHECY.

One subject that separates the Bible from every other book is prophecy. No other book predicts the future as does God's Word. The prophecies are precise. Many times they are hundreds, even thousands of years in advance. Without exception these prophecies are fulfilled to the smallest detail!

The Bible is a book of prophecy.

In the Old Testament there are 17 prophetic books: Lamentations, Jeremiah, Daniel, Isaiah, Ezekiel, Hosea, Zephaniah, Haggai, Amos, Zechariah, Micah, Obadiah, Nahum, Habakkuk, Jonah, Joel, and Malachi. These books contain "near prophecies" for Israel and "far prophecies" for the end times. Many other books in the Bible contain prophecy as well.

I'm not sure who wrote it, but I found this old excerpt that explains Bible prophecy succinctly.

"The Bible is the ONLY volume ever produced which contains a large amount of PROPHECIES accurately predicting the future of individual nations, peoples, cities, and the coming of One Who was to be the Messiah! Although the ancient world had many different devices for determining the future, NOWHERE in all of Greek and Latin literature can there be found ANY real specific prophecy of a great Historic event to come in the distant future. But the BIBLE is FULL of countless, detailed, specific prophecies, all of which have been miraculously FULFILLED and come true--except, of course, the final ENDTIME prophecies which are either to be fulfilled in the near future or are coming to pass right NOW!"

Consider one of the many prophecies that have be fulfilled in the smallest detail.

"A prophecy in Ezekiel 26:1-6 reads, ". . . the word of the LORD came unto me, saying. . . Behold, I am against thee, O Tyrus, and will cause many nations to come up against thee. . . And they shall destroy the walls of Tyrus, and break down her towers: I will also scrape her dust from her, and make her like the top of a rock. It shall be a place for the spreading of nets in the midst of the sea: for I have spoken it, saith the Lord GOD. . . "

Three years later, Nebuchadnezzar of Babylon surrounded Tyrus. But before he came, the people of Tyre escaped to an island, a half-mile offshore. After thirteen years of siege, the Babylonians "broke down her walls" and "broke down her towers", destroying the city on the mainland. By that time, the escaped people had re-built the city of Tyre on the island. And because Nebuchadnezzar had no navy, the city on the island remained untouched. Even though Nebuchadnezzar, destroyed the city, he didn't fulfill Ezekiel's prophecy. But 250 years later, Alexander the Great took the rubble Nebuchadnezzar's destruction left, and they "scraped her dust", the wood, rock and stubble from the destroyed city, and they built a causeway, like "the top of a rock". They marched on the rubble-causeway, into the island and destroyed it. And if you travel to site of old Tyre today - you'll see fisherman "spreading their nets" to dry on what was Tyre! Exactly, as Ezekiel prophesied around 586 B.C.! Over 2500 years before it happened!" - Terry Watkins

There were over 300 Biblical prophecies fulfilled in the person of Jesus Christ. They were written thousands of years before

Jesus was born! Precise, detailed prophecies such as; where He would be born (Micah 5:2), how He would be born, (Isaiah 7:14) how He would die (Psalm 34:20), etc. History proves, without a doubt, these predictions were fulfilled EXACTLY as the Word of God had prophesied, hundreds of years before.

"In the book, Science Speaks, mathematician and scientist, Peter Stoner, applies the rules of probability to these prophecies. The chances of just eight of these three-hundred prophecies being fulfilled are one in 10 to the 17th power - that's 1 in 100,000,000,000,000,000! In the book, Professor Stoner, illustrates:

Let us try to visualize this chance. . . Suppose that we take 10 to the 17th power silver dollars and lay them on the face of Texas. They will cover all of the state two feet deep. Now mark one of these silver dollars and stir the whole mass thoroughly. . . Blindfold a man and tell him. . . he must pick up one silver dollar . . . What chance would he have of getting the right one? Just the same chance that the prophets would have had of writing these eight prophecies and having them all come true in any one man. (Science Speaks, pp. 106 - 107)

Professor Stoner, then took 48 of these over 300 fulfilled prophecies. The chances of 48 being fulfilled are 1 in 10 to the 157 power - that's 1 in 10 with 157 zeros! Here's how he illustrates:

Let us try to visualize it. . . The electron is about as small an object as we know of. It is so small that it will take 2.5 x 10 to the 15th power of them laid side by side to make a line, single file, one inch long. If we were going to count the electrons in this line one inch long, and counted 250 each minute, and if we counted day and night, it would take us 19,000,000 years to count just the one-inch line of electrons. . . With this introduction, let us go back to our chance of 1 in 10 to the 157th power. . . Let us make a solid ball of electrons, extending in all directions from the earth to the distance of six billion light-years (the distance that light will travel at 186,000 miles a second in 6,000,000,000 years). Have we used up our 10 to the 157th power electrons? No, we have made such a small hole in the mass that we cannot see it. Now, one of these electrons was marked and thoroughly stirred into the whole mass; blindfold your man and ask him to find the marked electron. (The electron, in fact, is so small that it cannot be seen with a powerful microscope.) To the extent, then, that we know this blindfolded man cannot pick out the marked electron, we know that the Bible is inspired. (Science Speaks, pp 109 - 111)

And in case you think Professor Stoner's statistics are exaggerated or without scientific substance the "Foreword" of the book, Science Speaks includes an acknowledgement by the prestigious American Scientific Affiliation stating, "The mathematical analysis included is based upon principles of probability which are thoroughly sound and Professor Stoner has applied these principles in a proper and convincing way."

Professor Stoner concludes, "This is not MERELY EVIDENCE. It is PROOF of the Bible's inspiration by God - PROOF DEFINITE that the universe is not large enough to hold the evidence."

These are just a few examples (of thousands) that prove beyond any shadow of doubt that the supernatural hand of God was guiding the men who wrote the Bible.

What do you believe about Jesus Christ? Do you believe the record that God gave of His Son?

1 John 5:10–13

"He that believeth on the Son of God hath the witness in himself: he that believeth not God hath made him a liar; because he believeth not the record that God gave of his Son. 11 And this is the record, that God hath given to us eternal life, and this life is in his Son. 12 He that hath the Son hath life; and he that hath not the Son of God hath not life. 13 These things have I written unto you that believe on the name of the Son of God; that ye may know that ye have eternal life, and that ye may believe on the name of the Son of God."

Have you been born again?

John 3:3

"Jesus answered and said unto him, Verily, verily, I say unto thee, Except a man be born again, he cannot see the kingdom of God."

John 3:7

"Marvel not that I said unto thee, Ye must be born again."

If you have never accepted Jesus Christ as your Saviour, you can do so at this very moment. Receive Jesus Christ and believe on His name. Confess to God that you are a sinner who deserves judgment. Profess faith in the death, burial, and resurrection of Jesus Christ, the Son of God. Ask Christ to save your soul right now.

John 1:12–13

"But as many as received him, to them gave he power to

become the sons of God, even to them that believe on his name: [13] Which were born, not of blood, nor of the will of the flesh, nor of the will of man, but of God."

5. The Bible's Miraculous LONGEVITY.

1 Peter 1:23–25

"Being born again, not of corruptible seed, but of incorruptible, by the word of God, which liveth and abideth for ever. [24] For all flesh is as grass, and all the glory of man as the flower of grass. The grass withereth, and the flower thereof falleth away: [25] But the word of the Lord endureth for ever. And this is the word which by the gospel is preached unto you."

Since time immemorial, unbelievers have scoffed at the Bible and the enemies of God have tried to destroy it. The Bible is a threat to wickedness and tyranny.

Physical Attack

The Bible has withstood vicious attacks by its enemies as no other book. Many have tried to burn it, destroy it and outlaw it, from the days of the Roman emperors to some present-day anti-Christ countries. The Bible's very existence today and the fact that its teachings and truths have been preserved despite the countless campaigns and tirades against is proof the Book is SUPERNATURAL!

Jehoahaz became the king of Judah after his father Josiah was killed in battle. Jehoahaz was a wicked king. God commissioned the prophet Jeremiah to create a scroll containing the words of God. As the message spread throughout the kingdom, it came to the ears of the king. Jehoahaz commanded the scroll to be brought to him. The king disregarded the Word of God, cut it in pieces, and threw the pages in the fire.

Jeremiah 36:22–24

"Now the king sat in the winterhouse in the ninth month: and there was a fire on the hearth burning before him. 23 And it came to pass, that when Jehudi had read three or four leaves, he cut it with the penknife, and cast it into the fire that was on the hearth, until all the roll was consumed in the fire that was on the hearth. 24 Yet they were not afraid, nor rent their garments, neither the king, nor any of his servants that heard all these words."

Today, people who don't want to obey God seek to destroy God's Word and remove it from public view or discourse. Yet, the Bible remains!

Intellectual Assault

Since the enemies of God have not been able to destroy God's Word physically, they attempt to destroy confidence in God's Word. Satan's game plan has not changed since the Garden of Eden.

Genesis 3:1

"Now the serpent was more subtil than any beast of the field which the LORD God had made. And he said unto the woman, Yea, hath God said, Ye shall not eat of every tree of the garden?"

In France, Rationalism found a champion in Francois Marie Arouer—popularly known by his pen-name, Voltaire. Voltaire was a deist who produced several volumes overflowing with hatred for the Bible. No one in Europe did as much to destroy faith in the Word of God as Voltaire.

Eventually, the people of France rejected the Scriptures, tied a copy of the Bible to the tail of a donkey, and dragged it through the streets to the city dump, where it was ceremoniously burned. The author Coffman said, "since that time, the government of France has fallen thirty-five times."

Voltaire predicted that within a hundred years of his death (1778) Christianity would be swept from existence and pass into history. Yet, two centuries later rare is the person who owns a copy of Voltaire's writings, while almost every home is adorned with a Bible. When Voltaire died, his house was purchased by the French Bible Society where they printed Bibles!

The Encyclopedia Britannica notes that Voltaire was "inordinately vain, and totally unscrupulous in gaining money, [and] in attacking an enemy." His final days were spent in agony. As an ex-Catholic, he loathed the idea of not having a "Christian burial." He even signed a confession begging God to forgive his sins—which his biographers claim was insincere (Brandes). When the composer Mozart heard of the skeptic's death, he wrote: "[T]he ungodly, arch-villain, Voltaire, has died miserably, like a dog—just like a brute. That is his reward" (as quoted in Parton 1881).

Intellectual attacks on God and His Word have used many names and come in various forms over the years, but they all have failed. Rationalism, Intellectualism, Atheism, Agnosticism, fake science, etc. will fail to destroy the miraculous Word of God! It is indestructible!

The Anvil Poem by John Clifford

Last eve I passed beside a blacksmith's door

And heard the anvil ring the vesper chime;

When looking in, I saw upon the floor,

Old hammers worn with beating years of time.

"How may anvils have you had," said I,

"To wear and batter all these hammers so?"

"Just one," said he; then said with twinkling eye,

"The anvil wears the hammers out, you know."

And so, I thought, the anvil of God's word

For ages skeptics' blows have beat upon;

Yet, though the noise of falling blows was heard,

The anvil is unharmed—the hammers gone!

6. The Bible's Miraculous LEGACY.

Have you ever considered the legacy of the Bible? No other book has so changed individuals and transformed societies. Consider the effect God's Word has on the world!

The Bible Brings Salvation.

Every person who has ever been saved is part of the legacy of God's supernatural Word. The seed of God's amazing Word is required for salvation.

1 Peter 1:23

"Being born again, not of corruptible seed, but of incorruptible, by the word of God, which liveth and abideth for ever."

The Bible Generates Faith.

Romans 10:17

"So then faith cometh by hearing, and hearing by the word of God."

The Bible Produces Spiritual Growth.

1 Peter 2:2

213

"As newborn babes, desire the sincere milk of the word, that ye may grow thereby:"

Every faithful preacher declares the Word of God. The truth of God changes lives.

The Bible Directs Churches.

Every faithful hurch is the protector and proclaimer of God's Truth in the Word of God. If a church is faithful to God's Word, it will accomplish God's work in the community.

1 Timothy 3:15

"But if I tarry long, that thou mayest know how thou oughtest to behave thyself in the house of God, which is the church of the living God, the pillar and ground of the truth."

The Bible Produces Revival.

Revival is a renewal of obedience to God. Therefore, we cannot have revival without God's Word. A study the great Hebrew revival that took place under King Josiah reveals the importance of the Bible in revival.

2 Kings 22:11–13

"And it came to pass, when the king had heard the words of the book of the law, that he rent his clothes. [12] And the king commanded Hilkiah the priest, and Ahikam the son of Shaphan, and Achbor the son of Michaiah, and Shaphan the scribe, and Asahiah a servant of the king's, saying, [13] Go ye, inquire of the LORD for me, and for the people, and for all Judah, concerning the words of this book that is found: for great is the wrath of the LORD that is kindled against us, because our fathers have not hearkened unto the words of this book, to do according

unto all that which is written concerning us."

Every major English revival since 1611 has taken place with the King James Bible.

God works through His Word.

Isaiah 55:11

"So shall my word be that goeth forth out of my mouth: It shall not return unto me void, But it shall accomplish that which I please, And it shall prosper in the thing whereto I sent it."

Every soul saved, every church founded, every revival conducted, every victory won for God Almighty is the legacy of His indestructible Word!

The Holy Bible is the only book God ever wrote. It is a supernatural book that is different than any other book on the planet.

The Holy Bible is supernatural in six areas:

- Reality
- History
- Accuracy
- Prophecy
- Longevity
- Legacy

Thank God Almighty for His supernatural Bible!

18

Supernatural Sight

Proverbs 29:18

"Where there is no vision, the people perish: But he that keepeth the law, happy is he."

Ezekiel 11:24

"Afterwards the spirit took me up, and brought me in a vision by the Spirit of God into Chaldea, to them of the captivity. So the vision that I had seen went up from me."

Physical vision is important. Spiritual vision is a matter of life and death. Learn how to get a supernatural vision from the Holy Spirit of God.

Vision is important. I am so thankful that I can see. As I write this chapter, I am looking at the computer screen. Now I am looking out my window down my driveway. This morning, when I woke up, I opened my eyes. Physical vision makes life so much easier.

Years ago, I attended a large church with many thousands of members. The congregation had a large blind ministry.

The pastor explained that when he was out of town in an unfamiliar hotel room, he would cover his eyes for a while so that he couldn't see. He would try to live as a blind man for an hour or so to remind himself of the difficulties of the members of his church without physical sight. It gave him compassion for them and helped him pray for their needs.

Blind people can be greatly used of God. Brother Kurt LaBouve is a blind evangelist that sings and preaches. He sang at one of our Spring Save New England Conferences and blessed the hearts of all who attended. He has difficulties that sighted people do not, but he is more joyful and useful for the Lord than many who can see.

There are worse things than being blind. Helen Keller was born blind and deaf. She became a hero to many because she overcame unbelievable obstacles to accomplish much good. She uttered a profound truth that has become a famous quote.

Helen Keller said, *"The only thing worse than being blind is having sight but no vision."*

Some have eyes but cannot see!

Ezekiel 12:2

"Son of man, thou dwellest in the midst of a rebellious house, which have eyes to see, and see not; they have ears to hear, and hear not: for they are a rebellious house."

The rebellious Israelites were in bondage in Babylon due to generations of rebellion. Jerusalem was destroyed. The walls were broken down. The temple had been demolished. The best of the people were marched as slaves to Babylon and the remnant were left in the once-promised land homeless and hungry.

None of that had to happen! All this death and suffering was because they had eyes, but would not see, and ears, but would not listen to the LORD.

In His letter to the church at Ephesus in Revelation chapter three, Christ counseled them to "anoint thine eyes with eyesalve, that thou mayest see." What a terrible thing to have ears that won't listen and eyes that refuse to see! Don't make that mistake.

Revelation 3:18

"I counsel thee to buy of me gold tried in the fire, that thou mayest be rich; and white raiment, that thou mayest be clothed, and that the shame of thy nakedness do not appear; and anoint thine eyes with eyesalve, that thou mayest see."

Do you have spiritual vision? Can you see the supernatural things that God wants you to see, or do you only see the physical world? Spiritual vision must be protected like natural vision.

Does anyone love going to the eye doctor? I confess that I hate going to the eye doctor. It is such a terrible experience. First, they put you a machine that looks like something Dr. Frankenstein would have used to create his monster. Then they keep switching these tiny lenses that make your vision worse while asking if you can see better. After that humiliation, they put drops in your eyes to dilate them for days. (Ok. It's not days, but it sure feels like it.)

After allowing you to wallow in your pain with dilated eyes, they take a special pin with a light on it to touch your eyeball. They say it is to check the pressure in your eyes, but I personally believe that this is a form of torture used by the CIA in black sites around the world.

Oh, but that is not all. In a final test of human stamina and will to survive, they place you in a chair for one final degradation. They tell you to put your chin on a rest and look at a light. With a malicious smile, the eye doctor waits for you to relax and then PFFFFFT!!!! They blow a puff of air into your already traumatized eye! After you recover from the pain, they smile and tell you they want to do it to the other eye... No thanks!

Ok, maybe it's not quite that bad, but perhaps you can feel a little bit of my pain? At least we can agree that most people don't enjoy going to the eye doctor, but we love to see. That's why we go.

When our vision gets blurry, we need glasses or contacts to correct our vision allowing us to see the world as it is in truth. Likewise, the Holy Spirit uses the Word of God to correct our spiritual vision. Only when we see the world through God's eyes can we have wisdom.

The Bible is like wearing a MONOCLE. Before glasses became cheap and easy to manufacture, it was more common to wear a lens over one eye. If someone had a hard time reading, they would simply look through the monocle to read. If someone had difficult time seeing items at a distance, they would look through the monocle when necessary.

Humans are physical and supernatural. We have a foot in both worlds. Typically, we see the world through the eyes of the natural. However, with God's help, we can choose to look through the monocle of God's Word to see supernaturally.

It seems that many Christians have lost their spiritual vision. Why? Let's liken the loss of supernatural sight to physical sight to learn some lessons.

Why no spiritual vision?

1. Natural sight can diminish with age. Sadly, some people act as if they have been saved too long. By that, I mean that they are too far removed from their salvation. They haven't visited Calvary in a long time. They are so involved in this world that their spiritual vision has clouded. Visit the Cross often. Never forget what a privilege it is to be saved from sin and Hell.

2. Vision is distorted when you get a foreign object in your eye. Jesus warned about pointing out the "mote" in someone else's eye while we have a "beam" in our own. It is difficult to see our own sins at times. Sin will distort your spiritual vision.

3. Tunnel vision occurs when your eyes lose peripheral vision only seeing what is directly in front of them. Don't get so focused on anything that you lose perspective of your place in the world and God's Kingdom.

4. Near-sighted people can only see what is relatively close to them. They have a hard time seeing what is far way. Spiritually, these are people so focused on themselves and their desires that they cannot see the consequences of their decisions. Eyes of faith can rely on God during the journey without seeing the destination.

5. Far-sighted people can see things at a distance, but items that are relatively close get blurry. These people have big dreams and ideas but can't see how to live for God today.

6. Some people can't see what they should because they are looking at wrong things. God will never disappoint you, but people will. Christ will never let you down. Keep your eyes on Him!

7. Some people cannot see because they simply have their eyes closed. Like someone who squeezes their eyes closed when afraid, some are too scared to see. Pain, fear, and overwhelm cause them to shut their eyes and wish for better days. Open your eyes in faith, friend. God will give you supernatural sight to see what is and what can be if you follow Him.

We need a supernatural vision from God like Ezekiel!

Ezekiel 11:24

"Afterwards the spirit took me up, and brought me in a vision by the Spirit of God into Chaldea, to them of the captivity. So the vision that I had seen went up from me."

Supernatural sight is not fueled by human ambition, vain desires, or deceitful lusts, but by the Spirit of God.

Joel prophesied that people would have supernatural sight when the Holy Spirit came. We saw this event take place in Acts chapter two at the day of Pentecost. Don't long for dreams and visions of old. Today, God leads us through His Word, His man, and His Spirit. Ask God for clear vision empowered by the Holy Spirit of God.

Joel 2:28

"And it shall come to pass afterward, That I will pour out my spirit upon all flesh; And your sons and your daughters shall prophesy, Your old men shall dream dreams, Your young men shall see visions:"

Consider three vital truths about supernatural sight.

1. Supernatural Sight Comes From God.

At our natural birth, we are given physical sight.

Psalm 139:13–14

"For thou hast possessed my reins: Thou hast covered me in my mother's womb. ¹⁴ I will praise thee; for I am fearfully and wonderfully made: Marvellous are thy works; And that my soul knoweth right well."

Think of the miracle of the human eye. God created the eye with a cornea and a retina. Rods & cones allow us to see shapes, colors, depth, and texture! Physical sight is an incredible gift from God.

At our new birth, we are given spiritual sight.

2 Corinthians 4:3–6

"But if our gospel be hid, it is hid to them that are lost: ⁴ In whom the god of this world hath blinded the minds of them which believe not, lest the light of the glorious gospel of Christ, who is the image of God, should shine unto them. ⁵ For we preach not ourselves, but Christ Jesus the Lord; and ourselves your servants for Jesus' sake. ⁶ For God, who commanded the light to shine out of darkness, hath shined in our hearts, to give the light of the knowledge of the glory of God in the face of Jesus Christ."

John 9:24–25

"Then again called they the man that was blind, and said unto him, Give God the praise: we know that this man is a sinner. ²⁵ He answered and said, Whether he be a sinner or no, I know not: one thing I know, that, whereas I was blind, now I see."

The famous hymn, "Amazing Grace," reminds us that we were blind, but can see now with eyes of faith.

"Amazing grace

How sweet the sound,

That saved a wretch like me!

I once was lost, but now I'm found;

Was blind, but now I see."

With supernatural sight, we begin to see the world differently. We can live in the power of the Holy Spirit seeing the world as God sees it. We can have wisdom, understanding, and discernment not available to lost people. In addition, God will make known His will to us as we seek His leading each step of the way.

Psalm 37:23

"The steps of a good man are ordered by the LORD: And he delighteth in his way."

2. Supernatural Sight Determines Possibility.

Blind people can do many amazing things, but their vision limits their abilities.

Matthew 6:22–23

"The light of the body is the eye: if therefore thine eye be single, thy whole body shall be full of light. 23 But if thine eye be evil, thy whole body shall be full of darkness. If therefore the light that is in thee be darkness, how great is that darkness!"

Notice the power of the eye! What you are looking at determines so much of your life.

Years ago, a sweet lady in our church gave a testimony that

I still think of today. Her and her husband were sitting on the sea wall in Narragansett, RI, looking at the ocean during a beautiful sunset. Suddenly, her attention was drawn to a few pieces of trash on the rocks at the bottom of the sea wall below their feet. She became angry that someone would litter in such a beautiful place. She sensed a gentle reminder from the Lord that her experience was determined by what she choose to look upon. She could look at trash, or she could look at God's creation in awe.

Life is that way. You can choose to look at stress or you can choose to look at God.

What are you looking at? Do you see burdens or blessings? Do you see obstacles or opportunities?

Jesus said, "As ye have believed, so be it done unto thee." If you think you can't, you're right. If you think you can, you're right.

Matthew 8:13

"And Jesus said unto the centurion, Go thy way; and as thou hast believed, so be it done unto thee. And his servant was healed in the selfsame hour."

What if you greatest problem isn't your:

- finances.
- situation.
- relationships.
- area.
- talents.
- connections.

What if God is doing exactly what you believe is possible?

What if your biggest problem is that you are looking at the negative instead of what God can do?

Your vision determines your possibilities. You are capable of so much more than you can imagine through Christ.

Fill your spiritual eyes with light and your whole body will be full of light.

3. Vision is a Matter of Life & Death.

Proverbs 29:18

"Where there is no vision, the people perish: But he that keepeth the law, happy is he."

Imagine a blind person driving a car. Would that be dangerous? Consider a blind person at the shooting range. Would you want to go?

What about a pastor leading a flock that has no spiritual vision?

What about a dad or mom rearing children with no supernatural sight?

What about a Christian entrusted to spread the Gospel with no spiritual perception?

What about a teenager or young adult who has no spiritual direction?

Without supernatural sight, lives are ruined, and souls are lost forever.

Every great work for God was accomplished by someone who saw what was possible with supernatural sight.

Get a vision from God for your life. Supernatural sight is not fueled by human ambition, vain desires, or deceitful lusts, but by the Spirit of God.

226

Without supernatural sight, lives are ruined, and souls are lost forever.

Determine to get a supernatural vision from God!

Perhaps you had a vision in the past and it has grown blurry. Go to the supernatural eye doctor called the Holy Spirit and put on the corrective lenses of the Bible.

With supernatural sight, you will see clearly and accomplish more with God than you ever thought possible.

What do you see today?

What does God want you to see?

Ask God for supernatural sight.

19

Supernatural Fellowship

Philippians 2:1–2

'If there be therefore any consolation in Christ, if any comfort of love, if any fellowship of the Spirit, if any bowels and mercies, 2 Fulfil ye my joy, that ye be likeminded, having the same love, being of one accord, of one mind."

Believers have the opportunity for supernatural fellowship with God and man. Learn how to access this incredible privilege through the Holy Spirit.

Fellowship is an old-English word used in the Bible. It is a vital part of the Christian life.

What is fellowship?

Consider this definition from *Webster's 1828 Dictionary.*

1. Companionship; society; consort; mutual association of persons on equal and friendly terms; familiar intercourse.

Have no fellowship with the unfruitful works of darkness. Eph. 5.

Men are made for society and mutual fellowship. Calamy.

2. Association; confederacy; combination.

3. Partnership; joint interest; as fellowship in pain. Milton.

4. Company; a state of being together.

Baker Encyclopedia of the Bible gives the following definition for Biblical fellowship.

"The essence of the Christian life—fellowship with God and fellowship with other believers in Christ."

In the study of Biblical fellowship, we learn that we have fellowship with the Sovereign, the Son, the Spirit, and the Saints.

Fellowship can be described by 3 words:

1. Relationship
2. Companionship
3. Partnership

Today, we will look at two important doctrines of fellowship WITH the Spirit and fellowship OF the Spirit.

Philippians 2:1–2

"If there be therefore any consolation in Christ, if any comfort of love, if any fellowship of the Spirit, if any bowels and mercies, ² Fulfil ye my joy, that ye be likeminded, having the same love, being of one accord, of one mind."

In Philippians 2:1, the Apostle Paul employs four irrefutable truths to beseech the believers in that city to unify. Unity is possible because of these amazing gifts imparted through Christ's sacrifice.

a. Consolation in Christ. This is comfort we find in Christ.

b. Comfort of Love in Christ. This is the comforting security we have in Christ's love.

c. Fellowship of the Spirit. This is our fellowship with God and one another through the Spirit.

d. Bowels and Mercies. This is the affectionate bond of believers through grace and mercy.

Paul declares the fellowship of the Spirit as an absolute of the Christian life. Are you aware of the vital doctrine? Are you enjoying the benefits of this supernatural fellowship?

There are two parts of our supernatural fellowship.

A. Fellowship WITH the Spirit. This is our fellowship with God through the Holy Spirit.

B. Fellowship OF the Spirit. This is our fellowship with other believers through the Holy Spirit.

I. Fellowship WITH The Spirit.

We must cultivate our relationship with the blessed Spirit. Consider the three elements of fellowship in our relationship with the Holy Spirit.

A. Relationship With The Holy Spirit

Supernatural fellowship begins with God. We have access to God through the sacrifice of Jesus Christ. Our daily relationship with God occurs through the Holy Spirit. In this age, the Holy Ghost interacts in a close and constant manner.

Ephesians 1:13–14

"In whom ye also trusted, after that ye heard the word of truth, the gospel of your salvation: in whom also after that ye believed, ye were sealed with that holy Spirit of promise, Which is the earnest of our inheritance until the redemption of the purchased possession, unto the praise of his glory."

1 Corinthians 6:19–20

"What? know ye not that your body is the temple of the Holy Ghost which is in you, which ye have of God, and ye are not your own? For ye are bought with a price: therefore glorify God in your body, and in your spirit, which are God's."

B. Companionship With The Holy Spirit

Ephesians 2:18–22

"For through him we both have access by one Spirit unto the Father. Now therefore ye are no more strangers and foreigners, but fellowcitizens with the saints, and of the household of God; And are built upon the foundation of the apostles and prophets, Jesus Christ himself being the chief corner stone; In whom all the building fitly framed together groweth unto an holy temple in the Lord: In whom ye also are builded together for an habitation of God through the Spirit."

i. The Spirit is Christ in us.

Colossians 1:27

"To whom God would make known what is the riches of the glory of this mystery among the Gentiles; which is Christ in you, the hope of glory: the Holy Spirit within

us in the conduit for our intimate relationship with God."

ii. The Spirit is our Comforter.

John 14:16

"And I will pray the Father, and he shall give you another Comforter, that he may abide with you for ever;"

John 14:26

"But the Comforter, which is the Holy Ghost, whom the Father will send in my name, he shall teach you all things, and bring all things to your remembrance, whatsoever I have said unto you."

John 15:26

"But when the Comforter is come, whom I will send unto you from the Father, even the Spirit of truth, which proceedeth from the Father, he shall testify of me:"

John 16:7

"Nevertheless I tell you the truth; It is expedient for you that I go away: for if I go not away, the Comforter will not come unto you; but if I depart, I will send him unto you."

iii. The Spirit of God gives us assurance of salvation.

1 John 3:24

"And he that keepeth his commandments dwelleth in him, and he in him. And hereby we know that he abideth in us, by the Spirit which he hath given us."

3. Partnership With The Holy Spirit

The Holy Spirit is our Partner in God's service. Without His power, we can do nothing eternal. My hands can only touch the physical. Spirit-filled hands dedicated to God's services can affect the eternal!

A. The Holy Spirit is our prayer Partner.

Romans 8:29

"For whom he did foreknow, he also did predestinate to be conformed to the image of his Son, that he might be the firstborn among many brethren."

B. The Holy Spirit is our soul-winning Partner.

Acts 1:8

"But ye shall receive power, after that the Holy Ghost is come upon you: and ye shall be witnesses unto me both in Jerusalem, and in all Judaea, and in Samaria, and unto the uttermost part of the earth."

C. The Holy Spirit is our Partner in the Christian life.

Ephesians 5:18

"And be not drunk with wine, wherein is excess; but be filled with the Spirit;"

II. Fellowship OF The Spirit .

All believers have the holy spirit in common empowering a special fellowship with supernatural closeness.

Just as the citizens of a town drank out of the same well in Bible times, all believers drink of the eternal spring of the Spirit.

1. Relationship With One Another Through the Holy Spirit.

Every believer is born through the same faith, in the same Saviour. We will go to the same Heaven. We have been indwelt with the same Spirit.

1 Corinthians 12:13

"For by one Spirit are we all baptized into one body,

whether we be Jews or Gentiles, whether we be bond or free; and have been all made to drink into one Spirit."

2 Corinthians 13:14

"The grace of the Lord Jesus Christ, and the love of God, and the communion of the Holy Ghost, be with you all. Amen."

2. Companionship With One Another Through The Spirit.

Believers are fellow travelers through this life.

Christ's churches are meant to be cities of refuge for all the His people. Because of the communion of the Holy Ghost, people of all creeds, colors, and cash flows can gather in harmony.

Spirit-filled people get along with each other.

In Acts chapter four, Christians from all demographic categories came together in unity during a time of tremendous persecution.

Acts 4:23–24

"And being let go, they went to their own company, and reported all that the chief priests and elders had said unto them. ²⁴ And when they heard that, they lifted up their voice to God with one accord, and said, Lord, thou art God, which hast made heaven, and earth, and the sea, and all that in them is:"

Acts 4:31–37

"And when they had prayed, the place was shaken where they were assembled together; and they were all filled with the Holy Ghost, and they spake the word of God with boldness. ³² And the multitude of them that believed were of one heart and of one soul: neither said any of them that ought of the things which he possessed was his own;

235

but they had all things common. ³³ And with great power gave the apostles witness of the resurrection of the Lord Jesus: and great grace was upon them all. ³⁴ Neither was there any among them that lacked: for as many as were possessors of lands or houses sold them, and brought the prices of the things that were sold, ³⁵ And laid them down at the apostles' feet: and distribution was made unto every man according as he had need. ³⁶ And Joses, who by the apostles was surnamed Barnabas, (which is, being interpreted, The son of consolation,) a Levite, and of the country of Cyprus, ³⁷ Having land, sold it, and brought the money, and laid it at the apostles' feet."

Do we need pain and suffering to follow their example? We have plenty of reasons to run to God today! If we plead with God in one accord, He will fill every one of us with the Holy Ghost. Then we can live boldly, witness fearlessly, and take care of each other generously.

Christians have more in common through God than we have differences.

Ephesians 4:3–6

"Endeavouring to keep the unity of the Spirit in the bond of peace. ⁴ There is one body, and one Spirit, even as ye are called in one hope of your calling; ⁵ One Lord, one faith, one baptism, 6 One God and Father of all, who is above all, and through all, and in you all."

3. Partnership with One Another Through The Spirit.

Believers are called to work together to win the world to Christ. No Christian is meant to be a one-man show. The Apostles were a blueprint of a team working under the headship of Christ to accomplish the will of God.

Church members work together to fulfill the will of God in a community.

1 Corinthians 3:9

"For we are labourers together with God: ye are God's husbandry, ye are God's building."

Philippians 1:27

"Only let your conversation be as it becometh the gospel of Christ: that whether I come and see you, or else be absent, I may hear of your affairs, that ye stand fast in one spirit, with one mind striving together for the faith of the gospel;"

When we get in the yoke with Christ, we learn of Him.

Matthew 11:29

"Take my yoke upon you, and learn of me; for I am meek and lowly in heart: and ye shall find rest unto your souls."

When we work together in the service of the Lord, we develop a bond deeper than natural friendship.

Remember that you are never alone.

Fellowship is a pleasant part of the spiritual birthright of every Christian.

We have fellowship with God through the Spirit.

We have fellowship with one another through the Spirit.

Walk with God and man in the Holy Ghost to enjoy this supernatural blessing.

20

Supernatural Joy

1 Thessalonians 1:1–7

"PAUL, and Silvanus, and Timotheus, unto the church of the Thessalonians which is in God the Father and in the Lord Jesus Christ: Grace be unto you, and peace, from God our Father, and the Lord Jesus Christ. ² We give thanks to God always for you all, making mention of you in our prayers; ³ Remembering without ceasing your work of faith, and labour of love, and patience of hope in our Lord Jesus Christ, in the sight of God and our Father; ⁴ Knowing, brethren beloved, your election of God. ⁵ For our gospel came not unto you in word only, but also in power, and in the Holy Ghost, and in much assurance; as ye know what manner of men we were among you for your sake. ⁶ And ye became followers of us, and of the Lord, having received the word in much affliction, with joy of the Holy Ghost: ⁷ So that ye were ensamples to all that believe in Macedonia and Achaia."

Everyone wants to be happy. Most people stumble blindly

through this life seeking for happiness. Unfortunately, very few wanderers know where to find it. Most look for happiness in unreliable people, unstable situations, and fleeting pleasure. Sins such as immorality, drugs, alcohol, the party lifestyle, and selfishness promise happiness but leave people empty and broken. Thankfully, God has provided a roadmap to happiness for His children.

Joy is a priceless benefit of the Spirit-filled life. Joy is gladness from God.

Joy is far superior to happiness. Happiness is gladness from happenings. Happiness is completely dependent upon circumstances.

For example, if someone gives me $100 that makes me happy. If I lose the same $100 that made me happy, now I am sad. It is eye-opening to realize that my happiness can be controlled by a piece of paper!

On the other hand, joy is completely dependent upon my relationship with God. I can have joy whether I have the $100 or not.

Joy comes from God.

> *Psalm 4:7*
>
> *"Thou hast put gladness in my heart, more than in the time that their corn and their wine increased."*

Joy Strengthens. Joy Sustains. And joy is available to every Christian.

If God wants you to have joy, then why don't you feel it? Why are you so down?

You must know where to get joy.

If you want water, you must find a faucet. Likewise, you must get joy from where God gives it. Get to the spout where the joy comes out!

Compare the faucet to a bottle of water. Someone can bring a little joy in your life, but it is far better if you learn to get joy for yourself.

The Holy Spirit is the never-ending fountain of joy. When we live in the power of the Holy Spirit, we have an endless supply of joy from God.

God's joy is available.

God's joy is sustainable.

Our experience of God's joy is directly related to our relationship with the Holy Spirit. Let's learn how the Holy Spirit can bring us unspeakable joy in this life.

Let's review some details about the Holy Spirit.

He Is part of the Godhead.

Matthew 28:19

"Go ye therefore, and teach all nations, baptizing them in the name of the Father, and of the Son, and of the Holy Ghost:"

The Holy Spirit is a person with thoughts, feelings, and a purpose.

Galatians 4:6

"And because ye are sons, God hath sent forth the Spirit of his Son into your hearts, crying, Abba, Father."

The Holy Spirit is a person. He has thoughts, feelings, and purpose like every other living being.

He is called the Holy Spirit or Holy Ghost because He has no physical form on Earth.

John 3:6–8

"That which is born of the flesh is flesh; and that which is born of the Spirit is spirit. [7] Marvel not that I said unto thee, Ye must be born again. [8] The wind bloweth where it listeth, and thou hearest the sound thereof, but canst not tell whence it cometh, and whither it goeth: so is every one that is born of the Spirit."

The Holy Spirit indwells the believer at the moment of salvation.

John 14:17

"Even the Spirit of truth; whom the world cannot receive, because it seeth him not, neither knoweth him: but ye know him; for he dwelleth with you, and shall be in you."

The Holy Spirit is the down payment of our salvation.

Ephesians 1:13–14

"In whom ye also trusted, after that ye heard the word of truth, the gospel of your salvation: in whom also after that ye believed, ye were sealed with that holy Spirit of promise, [14] Which is the earnest of our inheritance until the redemption of the purchased possession, unto the praise of his glory."

The Holy Spirit is our Comforter and Helper.

John 15:26

"But when the Comforter is come, whom I will send unto you from the Father, even the Spirit of truth, which proceedeth from the Father, he shall testify of me:"

The Holy Spirit is God in us. He is our link to the Father and the Son. He is God's Cconduit for all the good things God is doing in us.

No wonder the Holy Spirit and supernatural joy are linked. Let's learn how we can experience joy through the sweet Holy Spirit.

1. We receive joy when we are full of the Holy Ghost.

Acts 13:52

"And the disciples were filled with joy, and with the Holy Ghost."

We are commanded to be filled with the Spirit.

Ephesians 5:18

"And be not drunk with wine, wherein is excess; but be filled with the Spirit;"

What does it mean to be filled with the Spirit? If we are full of ourselves, we can't be full of God. However, when we humble ourselves and yield control of our will to the Holy Spirit, He can fill us and accomplish God's work in us and through us.

You can review the chapter entitled "Pursuit of Power" to study how to be filled with the Spirit.

As we said, the Holy Spirit and joy are linked. Consider another verse that teaches this vital truth.

Romans 14:17

"For the kingdom of God is not meat and drink; but righteousness, and peace, and joy in the Holy Ghost."

2. The second fruit of the Spirit is joy.

Galatians 5:22–23

"But the fruit of the Spirit is love, joy, peace, longsuffering, gentleness, goodness, faith, 23 Meekness, temperance: against such there is no law."

The fruit of the Spirit is a byproduct of the fullness of the

Spirit. Just as a healthy apple tree bears apples, a Christian with a healthy relationship with the Holy Spirit will express the fruit, or byproducts, of the Holy Spirit.

Joy is a byproduct of Spirit-fullness.

Also, we have joy and peace in direct proportion to our faith in God and our power in the Holy Ghost. Faith and power often go together.

> *Romans 15:13*
>
> *"Now the God of hope fill you with all joy and peace in believing, that ye may abound in hope, through the power of the Holy Ghost."*

3. We hcan experience the joy of the Holy Ghost despite our circumstances.

> *1 Thessalonians 1:6*
>
> *"And ye became followers of us, and of the Lord, having received the word in much affliction, with joy of the Holy Ghost:"*

Thessalonica was a chief city in Macedonia. It was the seat of Roman administration in the century before Christ. It had a magnificent harbor and was located on the famous Ignatian Way, and was an overland route from Italy to the East that ran directly through the city.

On Paul's second missionary journey, he won souls to Christ and founded the church in Thessalonica. Although he wasn't in the city long, the church flourished. Their willingness to believe the Word of God and turn from idols to Christ became an example to other Christians throughout the world.

Thessalonica was a pagan city of the highest order. Those who preached the Gospel and the Christians who believed it faced serious persecution and lived in affliction. Yet they found great joy in the Holy Ghost.

Likewise, we can experience the supernatural joy of the Holy Spirit despite our circumstances.

The Holy Spirit is God in us. He is our link to the Father and the Son. He is God's Conduit for all the good things God is doing in us.

Don't waste your life seeking the world's fleeting pleasure. Why settle for the counterfeit of temporary happiness when you can experience true delight in the eternal joy of God today?

The Holy Spirit and joy are linked. Do you want joy? Submit to God and be filled with the Spirit.

21

The Supernatural Armor Of God

We are in a spiritual war.

The battle lines are drawn. Sides have been chosen. The forces of good and evil collide in a furious battle for the souls of men. Are you prepared?

Soldiers going into battle wear specific gear and carry weapons for the task at hand. Armor and weapons are directly related to life expectancy in battle. How long will you last in spiritual warfare if you are not wearing the proper armor?

Let's learn how to put on the whole armor of God.

The Battle

Every day, there is a spiritual war raging around us. God's people are not spectators watching the battle from a safe distance.

We are on the front lines. We are in the danger zone.

Bullets are whizzing by our heads. Traps are laid for our

destruction. The enemy advances upon our position. One wrong move, and we can become a casualty of this spiritual war.

This may not make sense to you as you hear it. You are probably reading this in relative comfort. You don't hear gunshots or see the enemy, so you feel safe. You are not.

This warfare occurs on a spiritual plane that can only be seen with eyes of faith. The evidence of carnage surrounds us yet is often explained away.

You can be successful in this war, but you must do these two things:

1. Acknowledge your place in the battle. Denial won't stop the enemy. Happy thoughts and good intentions won't protect you from the Devil and his minions. You are in the battle whether you like it or not. You will either fight the good fight of faith or be destroyed.

2. Use the armor and weapons God provides for your protection and victory. A good general equips his troops with the proper tools for combat. Our Heavenly General has given you spiritual armor to protect you from the enemy and the weapons you need to prevail. Use them!

Ephesians 6:10–11

"Finally, my brethren, be strong in the Lord, and in the power of his might. [11] Put on the whole armour of God, that ye may be able to stand against the wiles of the devil."

God provides you with supernatural strength and might for the battle. You will need every ounce of them! You are not strong enough to stand on your own.

This daily conflict will require courage. Resolve to be strong in God, facing each day with Him.

The Enemy

The Devil is your enemy. He wants to destroy you.

1 Peter 5:8

"Be sober, be vigilant; because your adversary the devil, as a roaring lion, walketh about, seeking whom he may devour."

The Devil is a liar and deceiver. He is a murderer who lives to steal, kill, and destroy.

Satan's priority is to blind people to the glorious Gospel of Christ, ensuring their eternal suffering in Hell. He is going to Hell, and he wants to take as many souls with him as possible.

Once you trust Jesus as your Saviour, Satan cannot touch your soul so he endeavors to destroy your life. He seeks to distract you from God's plan and ruin your testimony. Above all, he is desperate to keep you from sharing your faith, helping others to be saved. He will do anything to keep you from winning souls.

Ephesians 6:12

"For we wrestle not against flesh and blood, but against principalities, against powers, against the rulers of the darkness of this world, against spiritual wickedness in high places."

The Devil is not alone. He has an army of fallen angels (demons) to help him in his work. When Lucifer rebelled against God, he deceived one-third of the angels to follow him. This cunning victory demonstrates the strength of his deceptive powers!

Satan's forces are well-organized, working in tandem with this world system. They conspire against you to incite your flesh into selfish rebellion. Remember the three great enemies of righteousness: the world, the flesh, and the devil!

Thankfully, God gives us the tools necessary for victory.

The Armor

Ephesians 6:11

"Put on the whole armour of God, that ye may be able to stand against the wiles of the devil."

The words "whole armour" came from the Greek word for "panoply." It represents the full armor of a heavily armed soldier. During the days of Paul, a Roman soldier was the perfect illustration of this truth.

Two other passages of Scripture mention the armor of God.

Romans 13:12

"The night is far spent, the day is at hand: let us therefore cast off the works of darkness, and let us put on the armour of light."

In this verse, the armor of God is called "the armour of light." God is light. It is fitting that the armor He provides for His children to fight the forces of darkness is made of light.

2 Corinthians 6:7

"By the word of truth, by the power of God, by the armour of righteousness on the right hand and on the left,"

Here the armor is called "the armour of righteousness." Is there anything else that can stand against sin and wickedness?

Also, notice that the armor protects on the "right hand and on the left." It defends our flanks. The right hand in the Bible often symbolizes our strengths and the left hand our weaknesses.

The armor of God defends the front and sides of the Christian soldier. It is a full armor!

However, the armor of God doesn't defend your back. There is no protection in retreat! Stay in the battle and stand in the evil day. Your spiritual armor is more than enough to protect you.

The armor of God is mentioned a second time in Ephesians 6.

Ephesians 6:13

"Wherefore take unto you the whole armour of God, that ye may be able to withstand in the evil day, and having done all, to stand."

Because we are in a battle facing a well-organized enemy, we must put on the armor of God to survive and win the victory.

Consider three truths regarding our supernatural armor.

1. The Demand of The Armor of God.

Ephesians chapter six gives us to reasons that demand our use of the armor of God.

A. To Survive

Ephesians 6:11

"Put on the whole armour of God, that ye may be able to stand against the wiles of the devil."

The word "stand" in this verse means to "abide, continue, or hold up." In other words, we need the armor of God to SURVIVE!

We cannot survive the onslaught of Satan and his armies on our own. We must use the whole armor of God.

B. To Stand

Ephesians 6:13

"Wherefore take unto you the whole armour of God, that ye may be able to withstand in the evil day, and having done all, to stand."

In this verse, the word "withstand" means to "stand against or oppose." This means that we can fight against the Evil One when we use God's strength and armor. We can do more than survive: we can win!

Victory is the goal! The goal is not survival, but victory!

However, on the worst of days, when everything goes wrong and all the forces of Hell attack, the evil day, you can still be standing when the dust settles.

2. The Duties of the Armor of God.

A. Protection of God's Armor.

Soldiers have worn protective armor since the earliest days of war. Armor could be constructed of everything from thick leather to shaped metal. Stronger materials increased the protective strength of the shielding.

God has given us indestructible armor that cannot be pierced when used properly. Satan has no weapon that can defeat the armor of God.

Isaiah 54:17

"No weapon that is formed against thee shall prosper; And every tongue that shall rise against thee in judgment thou shalt condemn. This is the heritage of the servants of the LORD, And their righteousness is of me, saith the LORD."

The only time the armor of God fails to protect us is when we forget to put it on!

252

B. Pieces of God's Armor

There are seven elements that make up the Christian's supernatural armor. Let's identify them.

1. The Belt Of Truth Protects The Loins.

Ephesians 6:14

"Stand therefore, having your loins girt about with truth, and having on the breastplate of righteousness;"

Read the explanation of "loins" from Eerdman's Dictionary of the Bible.

Loins

The area of the body located at the hips or lower back. The loins were the place where the belt is worn (2 Kgs. 1:8; Isa. 11:5; Jer. 13:1), the sword hung (2 Sam. 20:8), and sackcloth placed (Gen. 37:34; 1 Kgs. 20:32; Amos 8:10). When quick movement was essential, the loins were the place where the garments were tied (Exod. 12:11; 1 Kgs. 18:46; 2 Kgs. 9:1); in this capacity the expression "girding the loins" became an idiom for dressing for action or readiness (Job 38:3; 40:7; cf. Luke 12:35; Eph. 6:14; 1 Pet. 1:13). Great fear is often described as accompanied by discomforts of the loins (e.g., Ps. 69:23; Isa. 21:3).

The Hebrew word is usually associated with the genital area and thus, by extension, with progeny (Gen. 35:11; 46:26). As the area of procreation, the loins represent strength and vigor (1 Kgs. 12:10; Nah. 2:1; 2 Chr. 10:10).

Roman soldiers would wear a belt with a leather apron covering the loins. Sometimes this would include straps of metal hanging in front.

I believe the "loins" speak of our desires. Satan is very good at taking the normal desires of life that God has given us and perverting them into something wrong.

God offers this armor of protection to make sure that we don't get into lustful sin and succumb to the sinful desires of this world.

The loins must be protected by truth. God's Word is Truth.

John 17:17

"Sanctify them through thy truth: thy word is truth."

The truth of God's Word reminds us of the pitfalls of sinful desire. Everything in this world-system attempts to light an unlawful desire in you to get you to want things that are not rightfully yours. We must resist music, TV, movies, and popular culture with the Truth of God.

Natural desires must be kept for the right people in the right place at the right time.

Jesus Christ is Truth.

John 14:6

"Jesus saith unto him, I am the way, the truth, and the life: no man cometh unto the Father, but by me."

The ultimate goal of the Christian life is to be like Jesus. The impeccable character of Christ reminds us to stay pure and walk the righteous path.

Compare your beliefs and actions to the Bible. We must use the Word of God and the Truth of Christ to protect us from worldly lust and selfishness.

2. The Breastplate Of Righteousness Protects The Heart.

The breastplate is a piece of armor worn to protect the vital organs in the abdomen, including the heart, lungs, liver, stomach, and intestines. One shot to the chest can kill.

We put on the breastplate when we remind ourselves every day that through the salvation of Jesus Christ, we are righteous in the eyes of God. We are a new creature! Old things should be left behind as we walk in newness of life.

Satan is adept at getting us to feel like we are missing out because we aren't doing what the world is doing. He shows us the neon lights of the front door of sin, but he distracts us from the death in the back alley when sin is finished.

Doing right is more important that fleeting pleasure.

We must protect our hearts!

Proverbs 4:23

"Keep thy heart with all diligence; For out of it are the issues of life."

2 Timothy 2:22

"Flee also youthful lusts: but follow righteousness, faith, charity, peace, with them that call on the Lord out of a pure heart."

Choose to live daily in the power of the Holy Spirit striving to be like our righteous Lord. Strive after the by-products of righteousness including honesty, goodness, humility, strength, faith, and love.

3. The Preparation Of The Gospel Of Peace Protects Our Feet.

The feet are important to a soldier. They are the foundation of every offensive and defensive maneuver.

Battles have been lost because of widespread foot injuries among soldiers due to improper footwear and cold or treacherous terrain.

If a soldier can't stand, he can't fight.

The feet speak of our ways - our direction. We should protect our feet daily with the preparation of the Gospel of peace. What does this mean?

We must wake up every day with the intention to talk to people about Jesus. This desire protects our feet because it will keep us from going to wrong places or doing sinful things.

Psalm 40:10

"I have not hid thy righteousness within my heart; I have declared thy faithfulness and thy salvation: I have not concealed thy lovingkindness and thy truth from the great congregation."

Did you expect to talk to someone about the Lord today? Did you pray for openings and look for opportunities to win a soul?

If not, you didn't protect your feet!

4. The Shield Of Faith Protects Us From The Fiery Darts Of Doubt.

A Roman soldier carried a shield. It was usually constructed of wood covered with thick leather. It was invaluable because it could be moved to stop an attack on any area of the body. Also, it protected the soldier from deadly arrows.

Arrows were the bullets of the day. They could be fired from a distance and rain death upon unprepared soldiers.

God has provided us with a powerful shield as part of the armor of light. it is the shield of faith! Faith can stop the fiery darts of doubt and temptation that Satan hurls at us.

Faith is confidence in God. It is the assurance that God exists and will keep His promises!

Hebrews 11:1

"Now faith is the substance of things hoped for, the evidence of things not seen."

When we are under heavy fire from the enemy, the shield of faith will keep us safe.

5. The Helmet Of Salvation Protects The Mind.

Ephesians 6:17

"And take the helmet of salvation, and the sword of the Spirit, which is the word of God:"

The helmet protects the head. This includes the vitals of the eyes (vision), ears (hearing), mouth (speaking), and the mind.

This helmet of salvation represents the assurance of salvation.

1 Thessalonians 5:8

"But let us, who are of the day, be sober, putting on the

breastplate of faith and love; and for an helmet, the hope of salvation."

Christian hope is different than the human hope of of looking forward to good things. Christian hope is the assurance that God keeps His Word and His promises will be fulfilled.

If you doubt your salvation, you will never be able to grow and reach your potential for Christ.

The knowledge that you are a child of God who will be in Heaven with your Lord guides your thinking about every decision.

6. The Sword Of The Spirit Offers Offense & Defense.

Ephesians 6:17

"And take the helmet of salvation, and the sword of the Spirit, which is the word of God:"

The sword is a defensive weapon to parry other weapons. Also, it is an offensive weapon to attack the enemy.

The Sword of the Spirit is the Word of God.

7. Watching With Prayer Protects From Apathy And Weakness.

Ephesians 6:18

"Praying always with all prayer and supplication in the Spirit, and watching thereunto with all perseverance and supplication for all saints;"

The soldier's mantra is "Stay alert, stay alive."

Soldiers must remain vigilant or die in a surprise attack.

When God was choosing the 300 for Gideon, the final test was watchfulness. Those who drank while staying alert were chosen for battle.

Watchful prayer keeps us alert, empowers us for service, and protects our fellow soldiers.

3. The Desire For the Armor of God.

You should desire this divine protection every day. Who would want to go into battle unarmed?? Once we understand the importance of God's supernatural armor we won't want to live without it.

How do we put on the armor of God?

The Song, "Stand Up, Stand Up for Jesus," includes a stanza that says:

Stand up, stand up for Jesus,

Stand in His strength alone;

The arm of flesh will fail you,

Ye dare not trust your own.

Put on the Gospel armor,

Each piece put on with prayer;

Where duty calls or danger,

Be never wanting there.

You put on the armor of God through prayer.

As you are praying, visualize yourself putting on each piece of the armor. It doesn't take long, but it starts the day right and guides you all day long.

When you put on the armor of God in the morning, it protects you from spiritual attack and prepares you for supernatural battle. Don't start your day without it!

22

Worship In Spirit And In Truth

John 4:23–24

"But the hour cometh, and now is, when the true worshippers shall worship the Father in spirit and in truth: for the Father seeketh such to worship him. God is a Spirit: and they that worship him must worship him in spirit and in truth."

Worship is a vital part of the supernatural life.

Carnal Christianity has hijacked the idea of worship. Many people today believe that worship happens when the rock band starts to play.

If you don't understand worship, you cannot commune with God as He intends.

This message reveals what our Lord meant when He told the woman at the well that true worshippers must worship in Spirit and in truth.

If there are "true worshippers," then there must be false worshippers. Do you worship God correctly?

What is worship?

There are two meanings of the word worship in the Biblical sense.

> 1. To adore, honor, and reverence God with extreme submission.
>
> *Exodus 34:14*
>
> *"For thou shalt worship no other god: for the LORD, whose name is Jealous, is a jealous God:"*
>
> 2. To perform religious service.
>
> *John 4:20*
>
> *"Our fathers worshipped in this mountain; and ye say, that in Jerusalem is the place where men ought to worship."*

Worship in the Bible is a private act between an individual and God.

Our text identifies three kinds of worship:

> 1. The ignorant worship of the Samaritans.
>
> "ye worship ye know not what"
>
> The Samaritans had the first five books of the Bible. This mixed race of Jews and Gentiles would know something of Judaism, but their religion was mixed with paganism as well.
>
> 2. The intelligent worship of the Jews.
>
> "we know what we worship: for salvation is of the Jews."
>
> The Jews had the full revelation of God. Yet, through millennia of teachers and traditions, they had lost the

spirit of what God had taught them originally.

3. The Spiritual Worship of the Christians.

"The hour cometh, and now is, when the true worshippers shall worship the Father in spirit and in truth."

Our Lord paved the way to true intimacy with God through the indwelling Holy Spirit and the written Word of God.

There must be a harmony between God and the worshipper.

1. We must worship God in Spirit.

God is a Spirit.

2 Corinthians 3:17

"Now the Lord is that Spirit: and where the Spirit of the Lord is, there is liberty."

No man has seen the Father.

John 1:18

"No man hath seen God at any time; the only begotten Son, which is in the bosom of the Father, he hath declared him."

Every bodily appearance of God was Jesus Christ, the Son of God.

Colossians 2:9

"For in him dwelleth all the fulness of the Godhead bodily."

Old Testament appearances of God are known as Christophanies. A Christophany is an appearance of Christ before the incarnation or after the resurrection.

1 Timothy 1:17

"Now unto the King eternal, immortal, invisible, the only wise God, be honour and glory for ever and ever. Amen."

They that worship God must worship in spirit.

Man is a triune being with a body, soul, and spirit.

1 Thessalonians 5:23

"And the very God of peace sanctify you wholly; and I pray God your whole spirit and soul and body be preserved blameless unto the coming of our Lord Jesus Christ."

An unregenerate man's spirit is dead due to sin. When we are born again through faith in Christ, the spirit of man is resurrected.

Ephesians 2:1

"And you hath he quickened, who were dead in trespasses and sins;"

It is our spirit that communes with God. Only those who have been saved through faith can truly worship God.

Ephesians 2:8–9

"For by grace are ye saved through faith; and that not of yourselves: it is the gift of God: Not of works, lest any man should boast."

There must be harmony between God and the worshipper. Because God is a Spirit, we must worship Him in spirit.

Worshipping in spirit meant that worship was no longer limited to a certain place.

John 4:19–20

"The woman saith unto him, Sir, I perceive that thou art a prophet. Our fathers worshipped in this mountain; and ye say, that in Jerusalem is the place where men ought

to worship."

The question of WHERE to worship has long been disputed between religious sects.

The Jews believed they were to worship in Jerusalem as the Scripture taught.

In the revival of Hezekiah, he removed the high places (one of the only kings of Israel to do so) and personal altars demanding that all worship be done at the temple in Jerusalem.

An enemy king thought this was a bad thing and tried to use it against Hezekiah.

2 Kings 18:22

"But if ye say unto me, We trust in the LORD our God: is not that he, whose high places and whose altars Hezekiah hath taken away, and hath said to Judah and Jerusalem, Ye shall worship before this altar in Jerusalem?"

The high places were a constant thorn in the side of Israel. They represented a form of worshipping Jehovah but promoted self-willed worship and false doctrine. Groves and high places were also used to worship false gods.

God wants us to worship and follow Him as He has directed, not according to our own desires.

The Samaritans had their own place of worship not too far from Sychar.

Albert Barnes, in his commentary *"Notes on the New Testament,"* says, *"Mount Gerizim, but a little way from Sychar. On this mountain they had built a temple somewhat similar to the one in Jerusalem. This was one of the main subjects of controversy between them and the Jews."*

It is interesting that this sinful woman talking to the Messiah brings up a doctrinal dispute rather than dealing with her own sinful condition.

Sinners still do this today. The drunkard wants to debate the meaning of the Greek word for wine. The pothead misuses a Bible verse about herbs in Genesis. The backslider perverts the fact that God "looks on the heart," using it as a shield against rebuke.

Our Lord wisely teaches the woman at the well a great spiritual truth. God is not confined by space or time. He is everywhere all the time.

Therefore, our religious activity is not only confined to a certain place or time. How many children of God live one way at church and differently the rest of the week? This should not be so!

The Holy Spirit indwells our spirit and empowers us to commune with God.

True worship must be in spirit and through the Spirit!

Philippians 3:3

"For we are the circumcision, which worship God in the spirit, and rejoice in Christ Jesus, and have no confidence in the flesh."

2. We must worship God in truth.

John 4:23–24

"But the hour cometh, and now is, when the true worshippers shall worship the Father in spirit and in truth: for the Father seeketh such to worship him. God is a Spirit: and they that worship him must worship him in spirit and in truth."

Some believe the word "truth" in this verse simply means to

worship God in sincerity. Clearly, our worship of the Most High should be sincere. However, that is not the limit of what this verse means. Let's dig into the word "truth."

Popular culture accepts that truth is relative. In fact, they believe that everyone can have their own truth. No so!

The Bible teaches that Truth is:

- From God.

- Absolute.

- Universal.

- Unchangeable.

What does it mean to worship God in truth? Consider three facts about God's Truth.

Jesus Is Truth.

The Bible teaches that Jesus is the Truth. Truth is a Person. Jesus Christ is God's truth in human form.

John 14:6

"Jesus saith unto him, I am the way, the truth, and the life: no man cometh unto the Father, but by me."

Once again, the Scriptures teach that our access to God the Father is through Jesus Christ.

Romans 5:1–2

"Therefore being justified by faith, we have peace with God through our Lord Jesus Christ: By whom also we have access by faith into this grace wherein we stand, and rejoice in hope of the glory of God."

Ephesians 2:18

"For through him we both have access by one Spirit unto

the Father."

One must be born again through faith in Christ to worship God in truth.

Christ is the mediator between God and man. All worship must be through the Son of God. If you don't honor Jesus Christ, you cannot honor the Father.

John 5:23–24

"That all men should honour the Son, even as they honour the Father. He that honoureth not the Son honoureth not the Father which hath sent him. Verily, verily, I say unto you, He that heareth my word, and believeth on him that sent me, hath everlasting life, and shall not come into condemnation; but is passed from death unto life."

The Holy Spirit is the Spirit of Truth

God reveals His Spirit as the Spirit of Truth. The Spirit always speaks and promotes the God's truth.

John 14:17

"Even the Spirit of truth; whom the world cannot receive, because it seeth him not, neither knoweth him: but ye know him; for he dwelleth with you, and shall be in you."

John 15:26

"But when the Comforter is come, whom I will send unto you from the Father, even the Spirit of truth, which proceedeth from the Father, he shall testify of me:"

John 16:13

"Howbeit when he, the Spirit of truth, is come, he will guide you into all truth: for he shall not speak of himself; but whatsoever he shall hear, that shall he speak: and he

will shew you things to come."

The Holy Spirit and God's Truth cannot be separated. The Spirit IS Truth.

1 John 5:6

"This is he that came by water and blood, even Jesus Christ; not by water only, but by water and blood. And it is the Spirit that beareth witness, because the Spirit is truth."

Since the Holy Spirit is Truth, it cannot be separated from the Truth of God's Word.

The Word of God is Truth.

John 17:17

"Sanctify them through thy truth: thy word is truth."

We must worship God according to His Word. Self-willed worship is condemned throughout Scripture. Corrupt worship as illustrated by groves, high places, and mixed worship (God plus idols) have been condemned since the beginning of humanity.

There is no debate. If you want to worship God, you must come on His terms. You must follow His plan.

Anything else is a violation of His holiness and rejected as sin.

In Malachi's day, the priests were cutting corners in worship. God was not pleased and would not accept their offerings.

Malachi 1:8–10

"And if ye offer the blind for sacrifice, is it not evil? And if ye offer the lame and sick, is it not evil? Offer it now unto thy governor; Will he be pleased with thee, or accept thy person? saith the LORD of hosts. And now, I pray you, beseech God that he will be gracious unto us: This hath

been by your means: Will he regard your persons? saith the LORD of hosts. Who is there even among you that would shut the doors for nought? Neither do ye kindle fire on mine altar for nought. I have no pleasure in you, saith the LORD of hosts, Neither will I accept an offering at your hand."

God must be worshipped in Truth. His Truth. Any perversion of worship by preachers or people is unacceptable with God.

Some church services today look more like Baal worship than the holy worship of Jehovah. Some Christians do what they want when they want, living in wicked rebellion to God but add in a little "worship" of their own design to life and call it good.

So much of what is called worship today is in clear violation of the Word of God. Therefore, it is not true worship, but a wicked device of man and idol worship.

3. The Father is looking for such to worship Him.

God is looking for true worshippers. Can you sense the Father-heart of God seeking a relationship with His children?

Do you worship God in spirit and in truth? Now you can.

Be a true worshipper that God is looking for.

True worship is in spirit and in truth.

This means that all spiritual worship must be from our spirit, in the Holy Spirit, through Jesus Christ, in accordance with the Scripture.

Let's strive to live in worship to God every day in spirit and in truth!

23

Spiritual Gifts Are Your Superpower

Romans 12:6–8

"Having then gifts differing according to the grace that is given to us, whether prophecy, let us prophesy according to the proportion of faith; ⁷ Or ministry, let us wait on our ministering: or he that teacheth, on teaching; ⁸ Or he that exhorteth, on exhortation: he that giveth, let him do it with simplicity; he that ruleth, with diligence; he that sheweth mercy, with cheerfulness."

1 Corinthians 12:4–11

"Now there are diversities of gifts, but the same Spirit. ⁵ And there are differences of administrations, but the same Lord. ⁶ And there are diversities of operations, but it is the same God which worketh all in all. ⁷ But the manifestation of the Spirit is given to every man to profit withal. ⁸ For to one is given by the Spirit the word of wisdom; to another the word of knowledge by the same

Spirit; [9] To another faith by the same Spirit; to another the gifts of healing by the same Spirit; [10] To another the working of miracles; to another prophecy; to another discerning of spirits; to another divers kinds of tongues; to another the interpretation of tongues: [11] But all these worketh that one and the selfsame Spirit, dividing to every man severally as he will."

Every believer is gifted with unique abilities at salvation. These spiritual gifts become your superpower when you are filled with the Holy Spirit. Do you know your spiritual gifts? Are you using them for God's glory?

There is a distinction between natural abilities and spiritual gifts.

Natural abilities Vs. Spiritual Gifts

Every person is born with natural abilities. These competencies are built into our DNA when God decided the details of each life in eternity past.

Psalm 139:16

"Thine eyes did see my substance, yet being unperfect; And in thy book all my members were written, Which in continuance were fashioned, when as yet there was none of them."

Natural abilities vary with each individual. There is no one alive that has your unique mix of talent, potential, and personality. You are special!

Consider three types of natural abilities.

1. Athleticism - Some people are born with a body that is primed for physical superiority.

2. Singing - Some people are born with the ability to sing

272

well.

3. Intellect - Some people are born with great capacity for memory and comprehension.

While most people can improve in any of these areas with determined practice, undoubtedly some gifted people are born with an advantage.

These are natural abilities. Can you think of other natural abilities that are common today?

Some people are gifted with spiritual abilities like preaching and teaching.

Spiritual gifts are the superpower of every believer. Let's investigate the Bible to learn what they are and how to identify them.

1. Spiritual gifts are supernatural abilities empowered by God.

1 Corinthians 12:6

"And there are diversities of operations, but it is the same God which worketh all in all."

Notice that it is God that works, or empowers, spiritual gifts. God empowers all spiritual gifts in all Christians.

2. Every believer receives spiritual gifts at salvation.

1 Corinthians 12:7

"But the manifestation of the Spirit is given to every man to profit withal."

The Holy Spirit gives to each believer a different mix of spiritual gifts according to the will of God.

1 Corinthians 12:11

"But all these worketh that one and the selfsame Spirit,

273

dividing to every man severally as he will."

Let's highlight a few of these gifts, explaining what they are and how to use them.

There are three passages that speak of spiritual gifts in the Scripture. We will list the spiritual gifts and definitions from these passages.

1 Corinthians 12:4-11

Romans 12:6-8

Ephesians 4:11-12

Prophecy or Preaching

The supernatural gifting from the Holy Spirit to proclaim the Word of God with authority and clarity in order to correct or edify people.

Qualities – discerning, serious, bold and expressive, disciplined, decisive, convincing.

Ministry positions that align with the gift of Prophecy...

- Bible Teacher
- Bus Captain
- Children's Ministry Teacher/Assistant
- Discipleship Ministry
- Nursing Home Preacher
- Small Group Leader/Facilitator/Assistant
- Prayer Ministry Team
- Prison Ministry Preacher/Teacher
- Student Ministry Leader
- Sunday School Leader/Teacher

Ministry

The supernatural gifting from the Holy Spirit to care for, protect and lead others into a deeper relationship with God.

Qualities – nurturing, guiding, discipler, relational, leader, authoritative.

Ministry positions that align with the gift of Ministry...

- Bus Ministry
- Children's Ministry Teacher/Assistant
- Deacon
- Discipleship Ministry
- Men's and Women's Small Group Leader/Facilitator/Assistant
- Nursing Home Ministry/Visitation
- Nursery Worker
- Pastoral Care Team – Bereavement/Meals/Prayer/Visitation
- Student Ministry Leader – Junior High/Senior High

Giving

The supernatural gifting from the Holy Spirit to willingly donate money and resources for eternal purposes in other people's lives.

Qualities – good stewards, responsible, charitable, organized, private, people-focused.

Ministry positions that align with the gift of Giving...

- Church Events Planning Team
- Church Planting Team
- Community Work Team

- Emergency Response Team
- Fundraising Projects
- Hospitality Team – Usher
- Mission Trip Planning/Going
- Nursing Home Ministry/Visitation
- Outreach Events
- Pastoral Care Team – Bereavement/Meals/Prayer/ Visitation
- Prayer Ministry Team

Ruling Or Administration

The supernatural gifting from the Holy Spirit to strategize and direct the efforts of others, with careful oversight, along with the organization of plans to complete a common goal.

Qualities – dependable, goal/task-oriented, self-starter, delegates well, disciplined, planner.

Ministry positions that align with the gift of Administration...

- Bookstore
- Bus Ministry Leader/Captain
- Church Events Planning Team
- Church Planting Team
- Church Office
- Community Care Team
- Emergency Response Team
- Family Events Planning Team
- Fundraising Projects
- Library Coordinator

- Life Group Leader/Facilitator/Assistant
- Men's and Women's Small Group Leader/Facilitator/Assistant
- Ministry Coordinator/Leader
- Mission Trip Planning/Going
- Nursery Leader/Assistant
- Outreach Ministry Leader/Assistant
- Sunday School Director/Assistant/Secretary

Mercy

The supernatural gifting from the Holy Spirit to administer compassion and care for others who are hurting or suffering.

Qualities – empathetic, sensitive, compassionate, responsive, emotional, patient.

Ministry positions that align with the gift of Mercy...

- Addiction Ministry
- Bus Ministry
- Community Care Team
- Emergency Response Team
- Hospitality Team – Greeter/Information Center/Usher
- Nursing Home Ministry/Visitation
- Nursery Worker
- Pastoral Care Team – Bereavement/Meals/Prayer/Visitation
- Prayer Ministry Team
- Prison Ministry Team
- Sunday School

Exhortation

The supernatural gifting from the Holy Spirit to present truth or offer a rebuke to others in a comforting way, in order to help them make right decisions in their faith.

Qualities – motivator, supportive, trustworthy, discerning, practical, encourager.

Ministry positions that align with the gift of Exhortation...

- Bus Ministry Leader/Captain/Worker
- Children's Ministry Teacher/Assistant
- Discipleship Ministry
- Hospitality Team – Greeter/Information Center/Usher
- Life Group Leader/Facilitator/Assistant
- Men's and Women's Small Group Leader/Facilitator/Assistant
- Nursing Home Ministry/Visitation
- Pastoral Care Team – Bereavement/Meals/Prayer/Visitation
- Student Ministry Leader
- Sunday School

Helps Or Service

The supernatural gifting from the Holy Spirit to humbly assist, help or support, people or projects, without any need of attention for doing so.

Qualities – helpful, loyal, sincere, follower, good listener, empathetic.

Ministry positions that align with the gift of Service...

- Audio/Visual Team

- Bookstore
- Children's Ministry
- Church Events Planning Team
- Cleaning Crew Ministry
- Food Preparation
- Grounds/Maintenance/Repairs Team
- Hospitality Team – Greeter/Information Center/Usher
- Ladies' Ministry
- Life Group Host
- Moving Team
- Outreach Events
- Photography/Videography Team
- Vehicle Maintenance

Teaching

The supernatural gifting from the Holy Spirit to communicate Biblical truth in a clear and accurate manner, helping others to grow in their faith.

Qualities – analytical, self-disciplined, good communicator, detail-oriented, creative, methodical.

Ministry positions that align with the gift of Teaching...

- Bible Teacher
- Children's Ministry Teacher/Assistant
- Discipleship Ministry
- Ladies' Ministry
- Men's and Women's Small Group Leader/Facilitator/ Assistant

- Nursing Home Ministry/Visitation
- Prison Ministry Team
- Student Ministry Leader – Junior High/Senior High
- Sunday School Teacher

Pastor

The supernatural gifting of the Holy Spirit to lead, feed, and guide a local church with love and wisdom.

Qualities – committed, passionate, confident, people skills, wise, selfless.

Evangelist

The supernatural gifting of the Holy Spirit to help a pastor encourage and equip the church to win souls to Christ.

Qualities – influential, passionate, confident, bold, outgoing, enthusiastic.

Although the sign-gifts of the Holy Spirit ended with the completion of Scripture, we can still benefit of the vestiges of these gifts. Allow me to briefly define lesser understood spiritual gifts and how they apply to us today.

Word of Wisdom

The supernatural gifting from the Holy Spirit to see the world the way God sees it and explain it to others.

Word of Knowledge

The supernatural gifting from the Holy Spirit to know the truth and explain it to others.

Faith

The supernatural gifting from the Holy Spirit to have confidence in God in unique situations, strengthening the faith of others.

Healing

The supernatural gifting from the Holy Spirit to bring healing to the broken.

Miracles

The supernatural gifting from the Holy Spirit to accomplish tasks that defy natural wisdom or laws, bringing glory to God.

Discernment of Spirits

The supernatural gifting from the Holy Spirit to see beyond the visible, determining attitudes and intentions.

Diverse Tongues

The supernatural gifting from the Holy Spirit to learn and speak languages.

Interpretation Of Tongues

The supernatural gifting from the Holy Spirit to translate languages.

3. Spiritual gifts Are divine superpowers that help us profit in ministry and life.

1 Corinthians 12:7

"But the manifestation of the Spirit is given to every man to profit withal."

The word "profit" in this verse means to contribute. We can contribute to the ministry of the local church through our spiritual gifts.

Also, spiritual gifts can help us contribute to the common good as we use them to support our families. Find a career that employs your spiritual gifts and you will enjoy your job while making an excellent wage.

However, it is vital that we don't prostitute our gifts, using them to make money without service to the Lord. Allows put Christ first! You never go wrong by following Jesus.

When you operate within your spiritual gifts, you become a superhero with supernatural abilities.

You can do things other people cannot do. You can accomplish feats that would cause other people to fail.

Every believer must identify their spiritual gifts and use them within their local churches to bring glory to God. Spiritual gifts are your superpower when you are filled with the Spirit.

Find them. Use them. Enjoy them.

You are supernatural! Make the decision right now to live the supernatural life in the power of the Holy Spirit. If you do, your life will never be the same.

Conclusion

The book you hold in your hands may be the most important book, other than the Bible, that you will ever read. Not because of the author but because of the content.

If you sincerely and consistently apply the truths in this book, your life will never be the same. The Holy Spirit will make you a new person with new vision, new power, and new abilities.

Start right now.

Get on your knees. Bow your head and your heart before God. Confess every known sin. Apologize for ignoring the Holy Spirit. Beg Him to fill every part of your being as you yield your heart and mind to His leadership.

Begin a practice of asking God to fill you with the Holy Spirit seven times a day. Listen for His voice. Submit without question when He leads. Stay humble as this new power becomes evident to those around you.

You are supernatural. Welcome to the Spirit-filled life.

5 Steps To Heaven

1 John 5:13

"These things have I written unto you that believe on the name of the Son of God; that ye may know that ye have eternal life, and that ye may believe on the name of the Son of God."

Nothing in this life matters if you go to Hell when you die. Are you confident that you will go to Heaven? Do you know what the Bible says about securing your place in eternal bliss?

God made a way for you to know that you are going to Heaven by faith. You may be closer to Heaven than you think! Only five simple steps separate you from eternal joy with God in Heaven.

Walk the five steps to Heaven to settle your eternal destination.

1. THINK ABOUT YOUR SOUL.

Isaiah 1:18

"Come now, and let us reason together, saith the LORD: Though your sins be as scarlet, they shall be as white as snow; Though they be red like crimson, they shall be as wool."

When is the last time you considered the miracle of your existence? Why are you here? Why can you think, reason, and feel far above the animal kingdom? Are you a temporary cosmic accident with no true purpose? Is there nothing beyond the mysterious veil of death?

My friend, you have a lot to think about before you dismiss the afterlife and the eternal destination of your soul!

The Bible teaches that you are a special creation of God. You are here because He wanted you to exist. He has given you an eternal soul that will live forever.

Long after your body expires, you will still be, know, and feel. Your soul includes your personality and the part of you that is reading, understanding these words, and thinking about them right now.

Most people will enter eternity without ever truly thinking about their soul beyond popular quotes, philosophical bullet points, or preconceived ideas.

Take the time to learn what God says in the Bible about salvation before you wager your soul on anything else.

2. REALIZE THE PENALTY FOR SIN IS ETERNAL SEPARATION FROM GOD IN HELL.

The Law of Consequence is evident in your everyday life. When any law is violated there is a penalty. Whether you rob a bank or jump off a bridge, consequences will follow.

Our Creator not only instituted the laws of nature but also has given humanity a set of moral laws. The most basic of them are found in the Ten Commandments. Just as the laws of nature are in effect even if you don't acknowledge them personally, so are God's Laws.

When we break God's Law, it is called a sin. Sin separates us from God and condemns us to pay for our sin. Hell is the fiery eternal abode of those who die in their sin in everlasting torment. God doesn't want you to go to Hell. He made a way for you to go to Heaven when you die.

Revelation 21:8 b

"... and all liars, shall have their part in the lake which burneth with fire and brimstone: which is the second death."

Romans 6:23

"For the wages of sin is death; but the gift of God is eternal life through Jesus Christ our Lord."

3. UNDERSTAND THAT JESUS CHRIST DIED ON THE CROSS TO PAY FOR YOUR SIN.

If you owe money on your electric bill, the company doesn't care who writes the check as long as your account is paid. You owe a debt of sin. The price is death in Hell. Jesus paid your sin debt on the Cross.

When you accept His payment for your sin, your Heavenly account is marked "Paid in full" and your home is reserved in Heaven. When He arose on the third day, Christ proved that He was the Son of God and the Saviour of the world Who has power over death.

1 Corinthians 15:3–4 "

For I delivered unto you first of all that which I also received, how that Christ died for our sins according to the scriptures; And that he was buried, and that he rose again the third day according to the scriptures:"

4. SEE YOUR NEED OF JESUS CHRIST AS YOUR PERSONAL SAVIOUR.

You are a sinner who has broken God's Law. The wrath of God abides on you every moment until you accept Christ's payment for your sin.

However, this book in your hand is one more reminder that God is trying to get your attention.

God loves you and wants you to spend eternity with Him in Heaven. Nevertheless, if you reject His love, you will face His fierce wrath.

You have been warned! Don't refuse His repeated attempts to prove His love for you and save you. Do you really want to meet God Almighty face to face after rejecting His Son's sacrifice for you?

> *John 3:36 "*
> *He that believeth on the Son hath everlasting life: and he that believeth not the Son shall not see life; but the wrath of God abideth on him."*

5. TRUST CHRIST IN YOUR HEART AS YOUR ONLY HOPE FOR HEAVEN.

The Bible is clear that faith in Jesus Christ is God's plan for your salvation. Good intentions and good works can never overcome your sin debt. When you die, God will not let you into Heaven because you were spiritual, religious, or attended a certain church. You must believe in your heart.

Heart belief is more than a mental assent to the facts about the Lord Jesus. It is a personal confidence that Jesus Christ is exactly Who the Bible claims and that you are trusting Him with the eternal destiny of your soul.

The Five Steps to Heaven are summed up in the word – TRUST.

Romans 10:9–13 "That if thou shalt confess with thy mouth the Lord Jesus, and shalt believe in thine heart that God hath raised him from the dead, thou shalt be saved. For with the heart man believeth unto righteousness; and with the mouth confession is made unto salvation. For the scripture saith, Whosoever believeth on him shall not be ashamed. For there is no difference between the Jew and the Greek: for the same Lord over all is rich unto all that call upon him. For whosoever shall call upon the name of the Lord shall be saved."

Take the final step to Heaven right now!

If you believe in your heart that Jesus Christ is the Son of God Who died on the Cross for your sin, you should confess your faith in Him right now and pray asking Him to be your Saviour. He will see your faith, hear your prayer, and reserve your home in Heaven.

Dear JESUS, I confess that I am a sinner and cannot go to Heaven without You. I do not want to go to Hell. I believe that You are the Son of God Who died on the Cross to pay for my sin, that You were buried, and rose again.

Please forgive all my sin and take me to Heaven when I die. I am trusting You alone as my way to Heaven. Thank You for saving me. Help me live for You.

Amen.

Contact us at *me@paulechapman.com* if you chose to trust Christ as Saviour today. We look forward to rejoicing with you!

Appendix A:

34 Activities Of The Holy Spirit In The Christian Life

1. The Holy Spirit Invites us.

Revelation 22:17

"And the Spirit and the bride say, Come. And let him that heareth say, Come. And let him that is athirst come. And whosoever will, let him take the water of life freely."

2. The Holy Spirit Draws us.

John 6:44

"No man can come to me, except the Father which hath sent me draw him: and I will raise him up at the last day."

John 12:32

"And I, if I be lifted up from the earth, will draw all men unto me."

3. The Holy Spirit Convicts us.

John 16:7–11

"Nevertheless I tell you the truth; It is expedient for you that I go away: for if I go not away, the Comforter will not come unto you; but if I depart, I will send him unto you. 8 And when he is come, he will reprove the world of sin, and of righteousness, and of judgment: 9 Of sin, because they believe not on me; 10 Of righteousness, because I go to my Father, and ye see me no more; 11 Of judgment, because the prince of this world is judged."

4. The Holy Spirit Births Us

John 3:6–7

"That which is born of the flesh is flesh; and that which is born of the Spirit is spirit. 7 Marvel not that I said unto thee, Ye must be born again."

5. The Holy Spirit Adopts us.

Romans 8:15

"For ye have not received the spirit of bondage again to fear; but ye have received the Spirit of adoption, whereby we cry, Abba, Father."

6. The Holy Spirit Baptizes us.

1 Corinthians 12:13

"For by one Spirit are we all baptized into one body, whether we be Jews or Gentiles, whether we be bond or free; and have been all made to drink into one Spirit."

7. The Holy Spirit Indwells us.

John 14:17

"Even the Spirit of truth; whom the world cannot receive,

because it seeth him not, neither knoweth him: but ye know him; for he dwelleth with you, and shall be in you."

8. The Holy Spirit Seals us.

Ephesians 1:13

"In whom ye also trusted, after that ye heard the word of truth, the gospel of your salvation: in whom also after that ye believed, ye were sealed with that holy Spirit of promise,"

9. The Holy Spirit Reserves us.

Ephesians 1:14

"Which is the earnest of our inheritance until the redemption of the purchased possession, unto the praise of his glory."

10. The Holy Spirit Liberates us.

2 Corinthians 3:17

"Now the Lord is that Spirit: and where the Spirit of the Lord is, there is liberty."

11. The Holy Spirit Comfort us.

John 14:26

"But the Comforter, which is the Holy Ghost, whom the Father will send in my name, he shall teach you all things, and bring all things to your remembrance, whatsoever I have said unto you."

12. The Holy Spirit Teaches us.

John 14:26

"But the Comforter, which is the Holy Ghost, whom the Father will send in my name, he shall teach you all things, and bring all things to your remembrance, whatsoever I have said unto you."

13. The Holy Spirit Reminds us.

John 14:26

"But the Comforter, which is the Holy Ghost, whom the Father will send in my name, he shall teach you all things, and bring all things to your remembrance, whatsoever I have said unto you."

14. The Holy Spirit Guides us.

John 16:13

"Howbeit when he, the Spirit of truth, is come, he will guide you into all truth: for he shall not speak of himself; but whatsoever he shall hear, that shall he speak: and he will shew you things to come."

15. The Holy Spirit Reveals us.

John 16:13

"Howbeit when he, the Spirit of truth, is come, he will guide you into all truth: for he shall not speak of himself; but whatsoever he shall hear, that shall he speak: and he will shew you things to come."

16. The Holy Spirit Inspires us.

Mark 13:11

"But when they shall lead you, and deliver you up, take no thought beforehand what ye shall speak, neither do ye premeditate: but whatsoever shall be given you in that hour, that speak ye: for it is not ye that speak, but the Holy Ghost."

17. The Holy Spirit Fills us.

Ephesians 5:18

"And be not drunk with wine, wherein is excess; but be filled with the Spirit;"

18. The Holy Spirit Empowers us.

Acts 1:8

"But ye shall receive power, after that the Holy Ghost is come upon you: and ye shall be witnesses unto me both in Jerusalem, and in all Judaea, and in Samaria, and unto the uttermost part of the earth."

19. The Holy Spirit Emboldens us.

Acts 4:31

"And when they had prayed, the place was shaken where they were assembled together; and they were all filled with the Holy Ghost, and they spake the word of God with boldness."

20. The Holy Spirit Speaks to us.

Acts 13:2

"As they ministered to the Lord, and fasted, the Holy Ghost said, Separate me Barnabas and Saul for the work whereunto I have called them."

21. The Holy Spirit Sends us.

Acts 13:4

"So they, being sent forth by the Holy Ghost, departed unto Seleucia; and from thence they sailed to Cyprus."

22. The Holy Spirit Leads us.

Romans 8:14

"For as many as are led by the Spirit of God, they are the sons of God."

Luke 4:1

"And Jesus being full of the Holy Ghost returned from Jordan, and was led by the Spirit into the wilderness,"

23. The Holy Spirit Helps us.

Romans 8:26

"Likewise the Spirit also helpeth our infirmities: for we know not what we should pray for as we ought: but the Spirit itself maketh intercession for us with groanings which cannot be uttered."

24. The Holy Spirit Intercedes for us.

Romans 8:26–27

"Likewise the Spirit also helpeth our infirmities: for we know not what we should pray for as we ought: but the Spirit itself maketh intercession for us with groanings which cannot be uttered. 27 And he that searcheth the hearts knoweth what is the mind of the Spirit, because he maketh intercession for the saints according to the will of God."

25. The Holy Spirit Cheers us.

Romans 14:17

"For the kingdom of God is not meat and drink; but righteousness, and peace, and joy in the Holy Ghost."

26. The Holy Spirit Gifts us.

1 Corinthians 12:11

"But all these worketh that one and the selfsame Spirit, dividing to every man severally as he will."

Luke 4:1

"And Jesus being full of the Holy Ghost returned from Jordan, and was led by the Spirit into the wilderness,"

27. The Holy Spirit Matures us.

Galatians 5:22–23

"But the fruit of the Spirit is love, joy, peace, longsuffering, gentleness, goodness, faith, 23 Meekness, temperance: against such there is no law."

28. The Holy Spirit Strengthens us.

Ephesians 3:16

"That he would grant you, according to the riches of his glory, to be strengthened with might by his Spirit in the inner man;"

29. The Holy Spirit Unifies us.

Ephesians 4:3

"Endeavouring to keep the unity of the Spirit in the bond of peace."

30. The Holy Spirit Sanctifies us.

2 Thessalonians 2:13

"But we are bound to give thanks alway to God for you, brethren beloved of the Lord, because God hath from the beginning chosen you to salvation through sanctification of the Spirit and belief of the truth:"

31. The Holy Spirit Corrects us.

Hebrews 12:9

"Furthermore we have had fathers of our flesh which corrected us, and we gave them reverence: shall we not much rather be in subjection unto the Father of spirits, and live?"

32. The Holy Spirit Moves us.

2 Peter 1:21

"For the prophecy came not in old time by the will of man: but holy men of God spake as they were moved by the Holy Ghost."

33. The Holy Spirit Renews us.

Titus 3:5

"Not by works of righteousness which we have done, but according to his mercy he saved us, by the washing of regeneration, and renewing of the Holy Ghost;"

2 Corinthians 4:16

"For which cause we faint not; but though our outward man perish, yet the inward man is renewed day by day."

34. The Holy Spirit Quickens us.

Romans 8:11

"But if the Spirit of him that raised up Jesus from the dead dwell in you, he that raised up Christ from the dead shall also quicken your mortal bodies by his Spirit that dwelleth in you."

About The Author

Paul E. Chapman loves helping committed Christians reach their potential, increase their influence, and impact their world.

He has served as the pastor of Curtis Corner Baptist Church since May of 2004. He and his wife, Sarah, are blessed with three precious children. They live in a coastal community in the beautiful state of Rhode Island.

They have a passion to reach the lost Christ and to train God's people for the work of the ministry.

Sarah has had a unique blend of aggressive autoimmune diseases since 2008 that leave her bedbound 95% of the time in constant debilitating pain. Their family's testimony of faithfulness to God has been an encouragement to many.

Paul writes weekly on his website and uses his unique blend of talents for God through various ministries and enterprises.

Learn more at www.PaulEChapman.com.

thepaulechapman

More Resources Available
This Publisher

Mini-books

Ye Must Be Born Again

The Abortion Atrocity

Books

God & America

Just Say No: 40 Days To Victory Over Sin

The Beauty Of Salvation: Marvel At God's
Unspeakable Gift

Praying Sinners To Jesus: How To Pray Effectively
For The Lost

Winning Souls Step-By-Step: Your step-by-step guide to
win souls, bring guests to church, and baptize converts.

Blessed Assurance: 50 Bible Reasons You
Cannot Lose Your Salvation.

Made in the USA
Middletown, DE
15 January 2024

47493437R00176